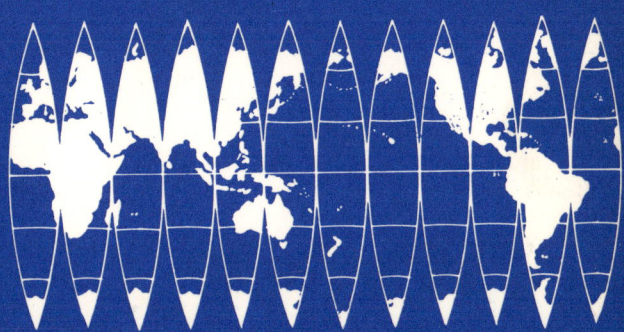

5-Gerken

Editor in Chief • PHILLIP BACON
Professor of Geography
Teachers College, Columbia University

Managing Editor • JOANNA ALDENDORFF

Associate Editor • PETER R. LIMBURG

Picture Editor • ROBERT J. GARLOCK

Picture Researcher • PETER J. GALLAGHER

Cartographer • VINCENT KOTSCHAR

Designer • FRANCES GIANNONI

Staff • JUDY KORMAN, BARBARA VINSON, KATHLEEN SEAGRAVES, JOHANNA GREENWALD

Special Section of Statistical Maps • RICHARD EDES HARRISON

Covers • RAY PIOCH

Maps on pages 3, 99, 194-5, 292-3, 294-5, 387, 484-5, 532, 533 are copyrighted by Georg Westermann Verlag. They are produced from the *Westermann Bildkarten Lexicon* by arrangement with Georg Westermann Verlag.

Complete List of Books

These books tell the exciting story of how people live in all parts of the world. You will see how men use the land for farming and industry. You will learn about mountains and deserts, oceans and rivers, cities and towns—and you will discover how the daily life of people in other countries compares with your own.

BOOK 1 • NORTH AMERICA

BOOK 2 • SOUTH AMERICA

BOOK 3 • EUROPE

BOOK 4 • ASIA

BOOK 5 • AFRICA

BOOK 6 • AUSTRALIA, OCEANIA
AND THE POLAR LANDS
WITH A SPECIAL SECTION OF
STATISTICAL MAPS AND INDEX

BOOK 3

EUROPE AND THE U.S.S.R.

BY HENRY HILL COLLINS, Jr.

THE GOLDEN BOOK
PICTURE ATLAS
OF THE WORLD
IN SIX VOLUMES

Illustrated with More than 1,000 Color Photographs and Maps

 GOLDEN PRESS · NEW YORK

© COPYRIGHT 1960 BY GOLDEN PRESS, INC. DESIGNED AND PRODUCED BY ARTISTS AND WRITERS PRESS, INC. PRINTED IN THE U.S.A. BY WESTERN PRINTING AND LITHOGRAPHING COMPANY. PUBLISHED BY GOLDEN PRESS, INC., ROCKEFELLER CENTER, NEW YORK 20, N. Y.

THIS IS EUROPE

Europe is the second smallest of the seven continents. Actually, it is a western peninsula of Asia. Geographers often speak of Europe and Asia together as Eurasia.

The eastern and southeastern limits of Europe are the Ural and Caucasus mountains in the Soviet Union. The waters of the Black and Mediterranean seas border the continent to the south. The Atlantic and Arctic oceans surround it to the west and north.

Although small, Europe has been very important in the history of mankind. Western civilization arose there and spread to North America, South America, and Australia. And European influence has been felt over the rest of the world.

Europe has more people—560,000,000—than any other continent except Asia. In places the land is very thickly settled. There are more people on each square mile of land in Europe than there are in any other continent.

For its size Europe has the longest coastline of any continent. If you look at the map, you will see that it has many bodies of water that are largely surrounded by land. This is true of the Mediterranean, Adriatic, Aegean, Black, North, and Baltic Seas.

As a result Europeans have been greatly influenced by salt water. Where the land, as in mountainous areas, has yielded a scanty living, people have gotten their food from the sea. At many places along the coasts they have become boatbuilders, shippers, and sailors, and engaged in foreign trade.

Europe has a great many mountains. The northern parts of Scotland and Finland, and almost all of Iceland, Wales, and Norway are rugged lands. To the south, on the continent, are the Alps, the Pyrenees, the Apennines, and the Carpathians. There are still more mountains in

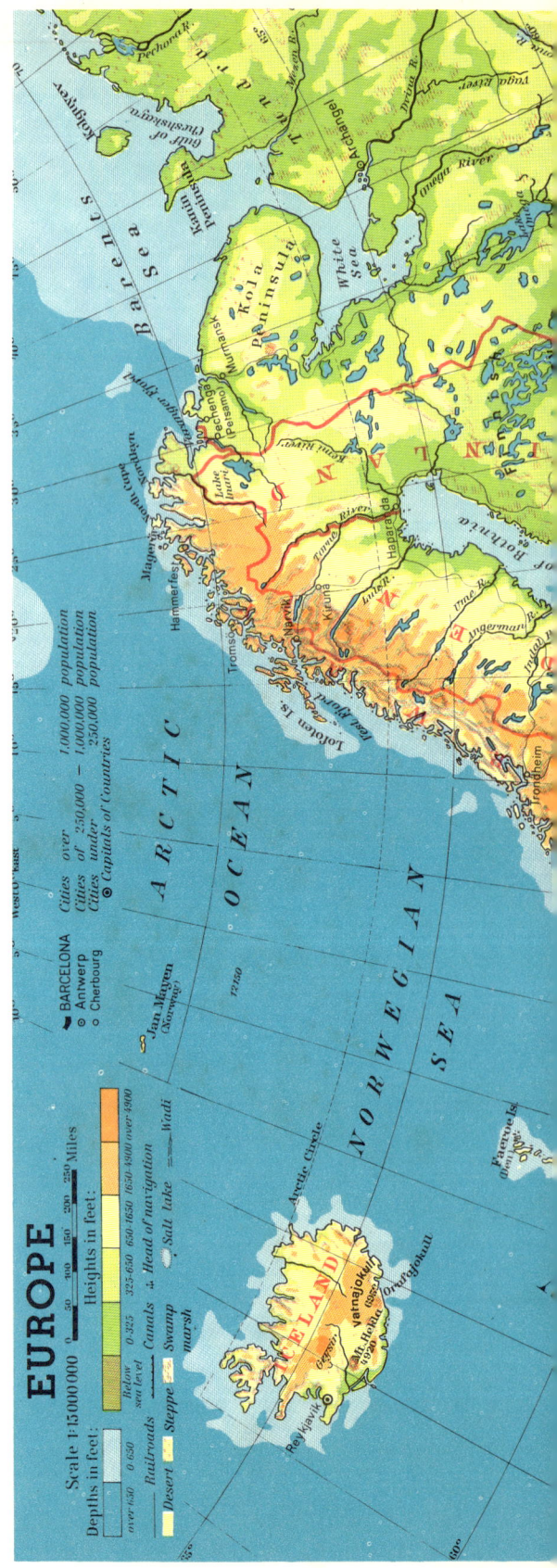

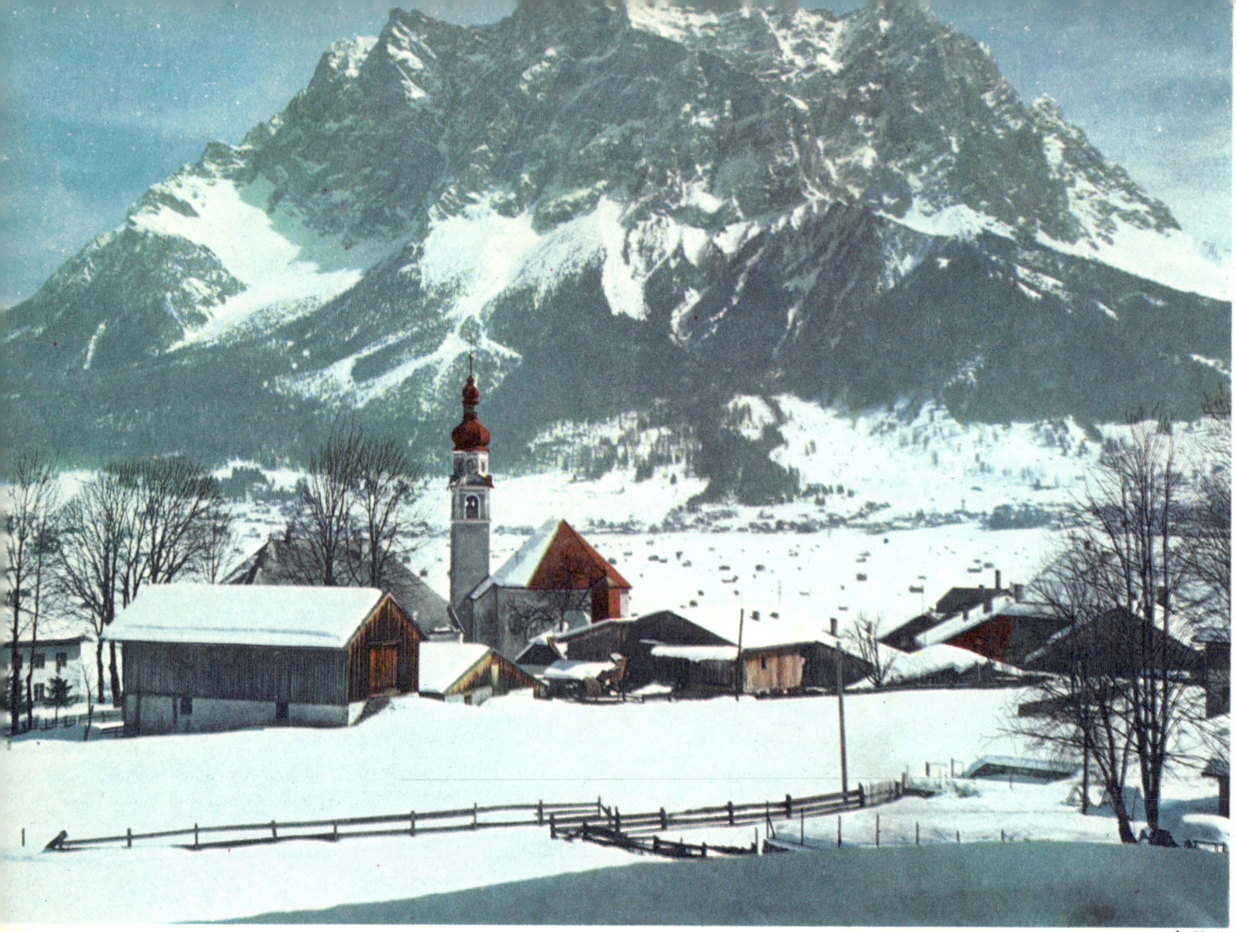

A. Modl

The Zugspitze, Germany's highest mountain, towers over this typical Alpine farmhouse.

Fertile plains and navigable rivers like the Seine, in France, are typical of western Europe.

Courtesy of TWA—Trans World Airlines

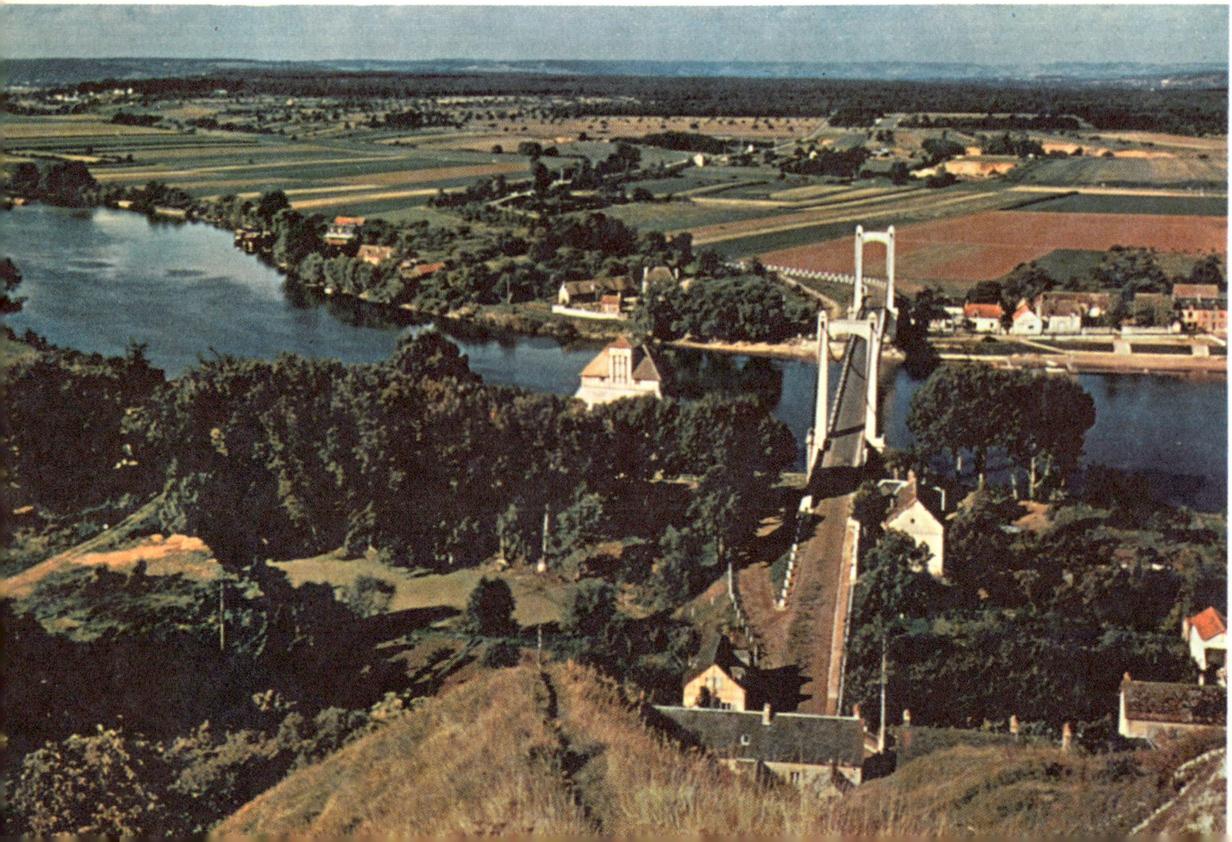

Norway's fiords were gouged out by glaciers in the Ice Age. This is the cliff-lined Sogne Fiord.

the Balkan countries of Yugoslavia, Albania, Bulgaria, and Greece.

In mountainous areas population is sparse, agriculture is difficult, and people are often poor. The chief occupations are grazing, forestry, or—where there are minerals—mining.

Mountains and seas have shut off the peninsulas of Spain, Italy, and the Balkans from each other and from the rest of Europe. This isolation has encouraged the development of different nations and cultures. This accounts in part for the great variety among the European peoples, and for the wars and political changes that have disturbed the continent since the days of Rome.

Much of the middle of Europe is a flat or gently rolling plain. This central European lowland stretches from the Atlantic Ocean through France, the Low Countries (Belgium and Holland), northern Germany, Poland, and the Soviet Union to the Urals. Travel on it is relatively easy. It has been a highway for warriors for thousands of years. It is also a land of great fertility. The eastern portion of it has been called "Europe's breadbasket."

Europe has three great rivers west of the Soviet Union. The longest, the Danube, flows east from the Black Forest in southwestern Germany through Germany, Austria, Hungary, Yugoslavia, and Romania into the Black Sea. The Rhone flows from the Alps in Switzerland through France into the Mediterranean. The Rhine flows northwest through West Germany and the Netherlands into the North Sea. These and many other European rivers are navigable. They are also easy to bridge, so they do not form serious barriers to communication.

Level farmlands, a parklike landscape, and an ancient church are typical of southern England.

Europe has many natural resources. There are vast beds of coal in England and Wales, in the Ruhr Valley and the Saar Valley in Germany, in the Silesian part of Poland, and in Czechoslovakia. Iron ore is found in England, France, Sweden, Luxembourg, and West Germany. Coal and iron ore are the bases of an industrial civilization.

The greatest oil fields in Europe are in Romania. Otherwise Europe is rather poor

Ernst Kleinberg—Shostal

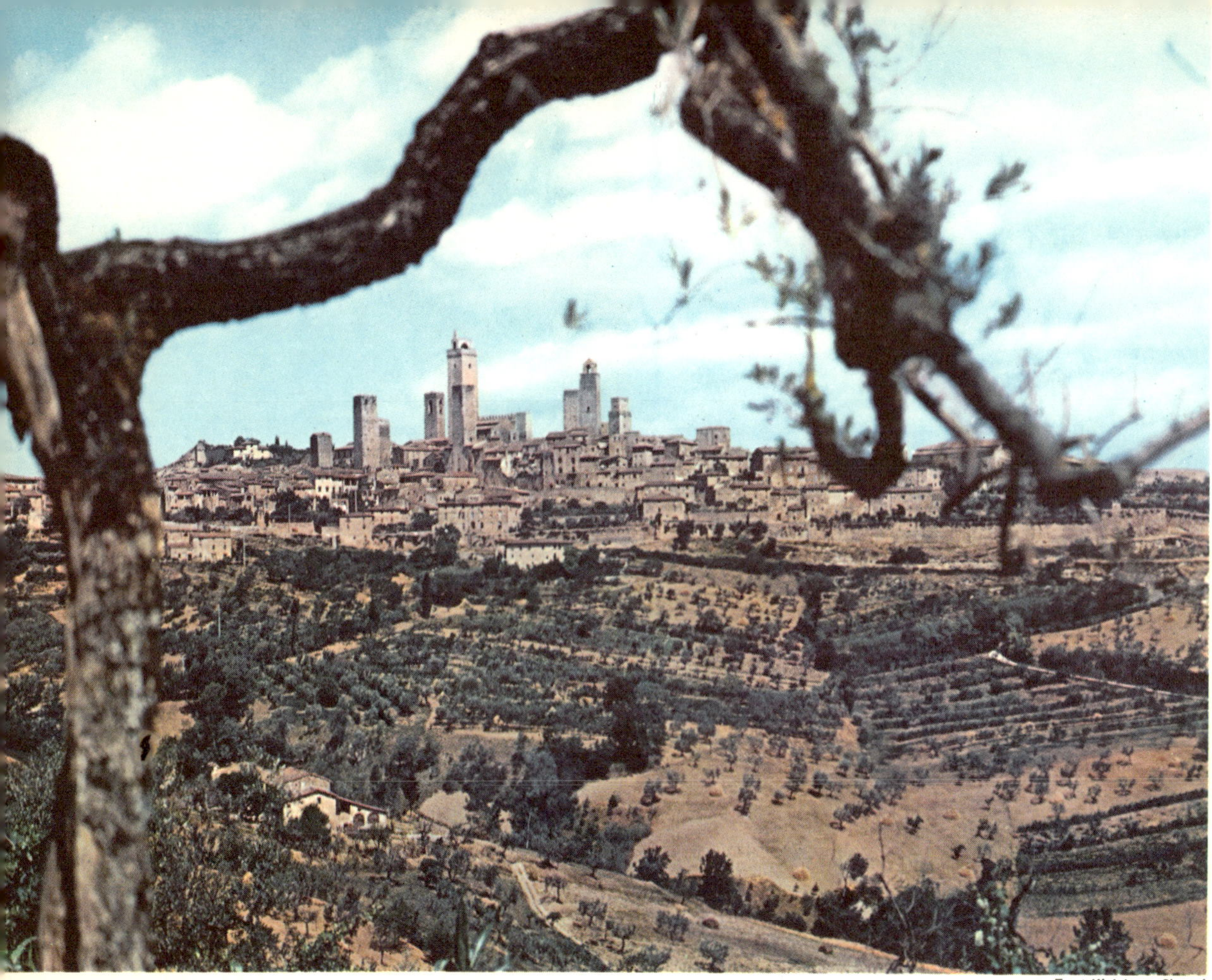

San Gimignano is one of the best preserved towns in Italy. Some buildings date from before 1300.

in oil. Ample hydroelectric power is produced from streams in the Alps and Pyrenees and the mountains of Scandinavia. Many other streams and rivers are still awaiting hydroelectric development. There are deposits of uranium ore in Czechoslovakia. Uranium is needed for the production of atomic power.

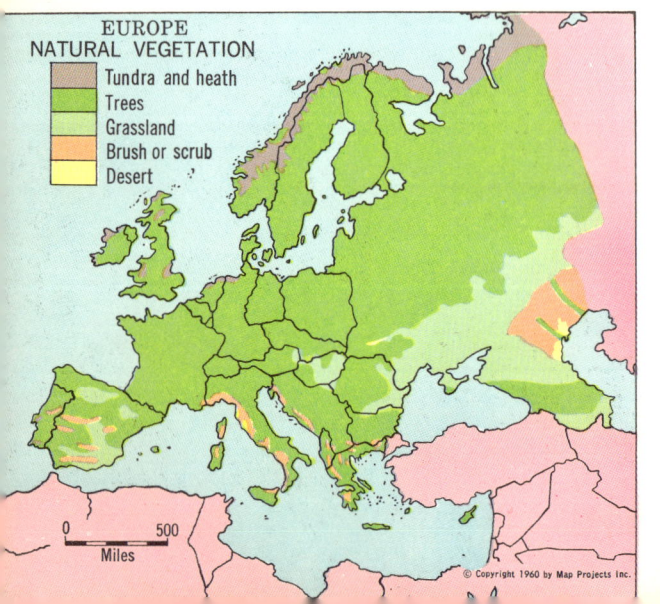

EUROPE
NATURAL VEGETATION
Tundra and heath
Trees
Grassland
Brush or scrub
Desert
0
500
Miles
© Copyright 1960 by Map Projects Inc.

Valuable mines of other minerals occur in different parts of Europe, such as Spain and Yugoslavia. Northern and Western Europe have large forest resources. The surrounding seas are rich in fish. All these natural resources have helped Europe gain a leading position in the world.

In the centuries just before the Christian Era the city-states of Greece were the strongest powers of Europe. They enjoyed the finest civilization man had ever known up to that time.

Rome followed Greece as the leader of the ancient world, conquering Europe as far as the Rhine and Danube rivers, as well as portions of Africa and Asia. From Scotland to the Black Sea there was one government, as there has not been since.

Grapes are grown on the gentle, sunny slopes along the Danube River in Austria.

The Roman armies kept the tribes of "barbarians," as the Romans called the peoples of the east and north, from pushing into the Roman Empire from Asia and northern Europe. Finally the armies of Rome were unable to hold back the invaders. For a variety of reasons her civilization fell. Her people fought and mingled with the newcomers.

Over the centuries the level plains attracted new tribes into Europe from Asia. The barrier mountains offered protection to settlers that had come before. Thus the plains and mountains help account for the many different peoples, languages, and nations in Europe. The long and protected coastline encouraged navigation and commerce. Great deposits of coal and iron aided in the industrialization of Europe in the 1800's. All these things helped make European nations in the early twentieth century the leading trading and empire-building countries in the world.

The ruins of the Temple of Apollo at Delphi are reminders of the glory of Greece's ancient past.

Mild winters, sunny summers, and the Mediterranean Sea make the Riviera a year-round resort.

Richard Zimmerman—Shostal

Herbert Knapp

Ray Gardner—Philip D. Gendreau

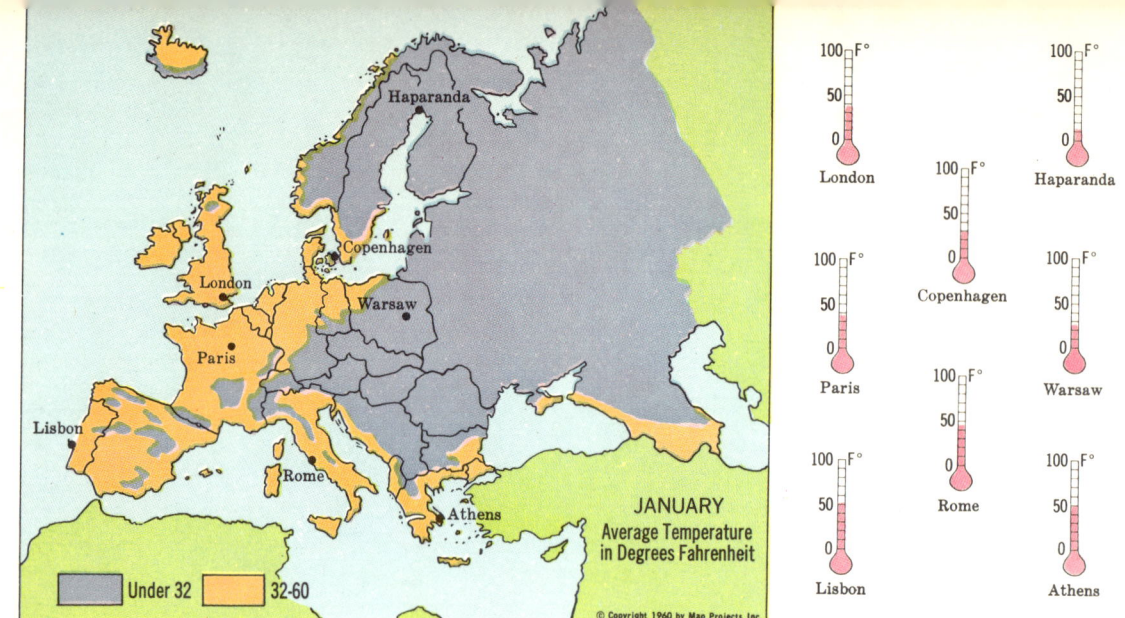

CLIMATE

Most of Europe lies in the same latitudes as Canada. Only such Southern European cities as Madrid and Rome are near the same latitude as New York.

Despite this northerly location, the climate of Europe is moderate. This is because of the North Atlantic Drift, part of the great ocean current of the Gulf Stream, which comes from the tropics and flows up along the Atlantic coast of North America.

Much of this warm current continues northeastward past Iceland, Ireland, and Scotland, and on up the west coast of Scandinavia.

Westerly winds blowing over these warm waters give the west coast of Europe and the British Isles mild winters, cool summers, and lots of rain. This is good for agriculture and human activity. However, persons who are accustomed to a drier climate often complain about the dampness and lack of sunshine.

Central Europe has cool winters, warm summers, and ample rainfall for crops. This climate is midway between the moderate climate of Western Europe and the more extreme climate of Eastern Europe.

Eastern Europe has cold winters, hot summers, and little rain. These features

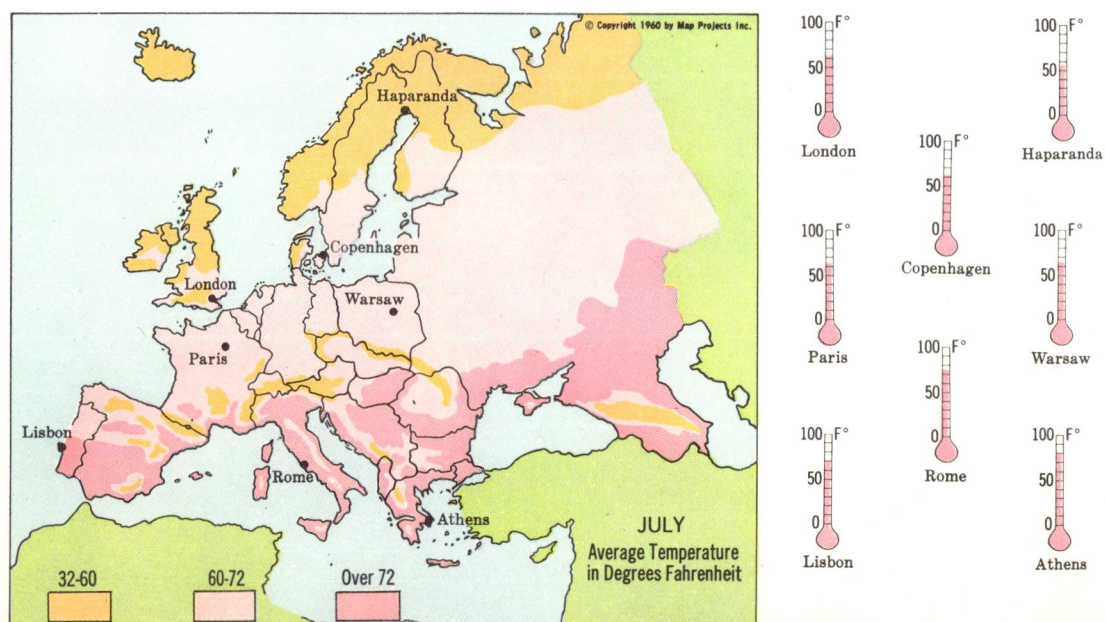

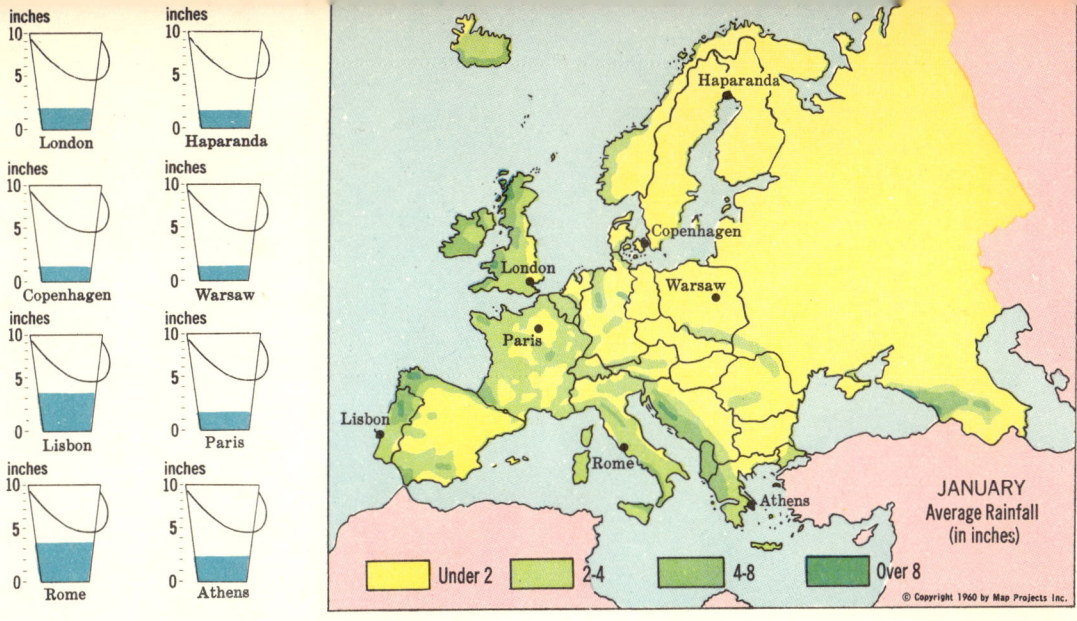

of a true continental climate become more marked as one goes eastward and away from the moisture and moderating influence of the ocean. Agriculture in general is not as productive as it is farther west.

Along the Mediterranean, and throughout Italy and Greece, the winters are mild and sunny, with some rain. Spring and fall are slightly warmer. Summers are hot and dry. The growing season is long, but summer droughts sometimes cause crop failures. The winter climate, however, is so delightful that it has made the Mediterranean coast a popular winter resort.

The only really dry regions in Europe are in central Spain, eastern Greece, and southern Russia. These areas are cold in winter, hot in summer, and have a very low rainfall.

On the tundra, or treeless region, of the far north, long cold winters alternate with short cool summers. Beyond the Arctic Circle the sun never rises for days or weeks in winter. And in summer for an equal time it never sets. In very dry or very cold regions agriculture is poor and population is limited.

The greater part of Europe, however has from 20 to 40 inches of rain a year. The climate generally is good for agriculture, and healthy and stimulating for human beings. This is one of the reasons why the nations of Europe have played such an important part in the world.

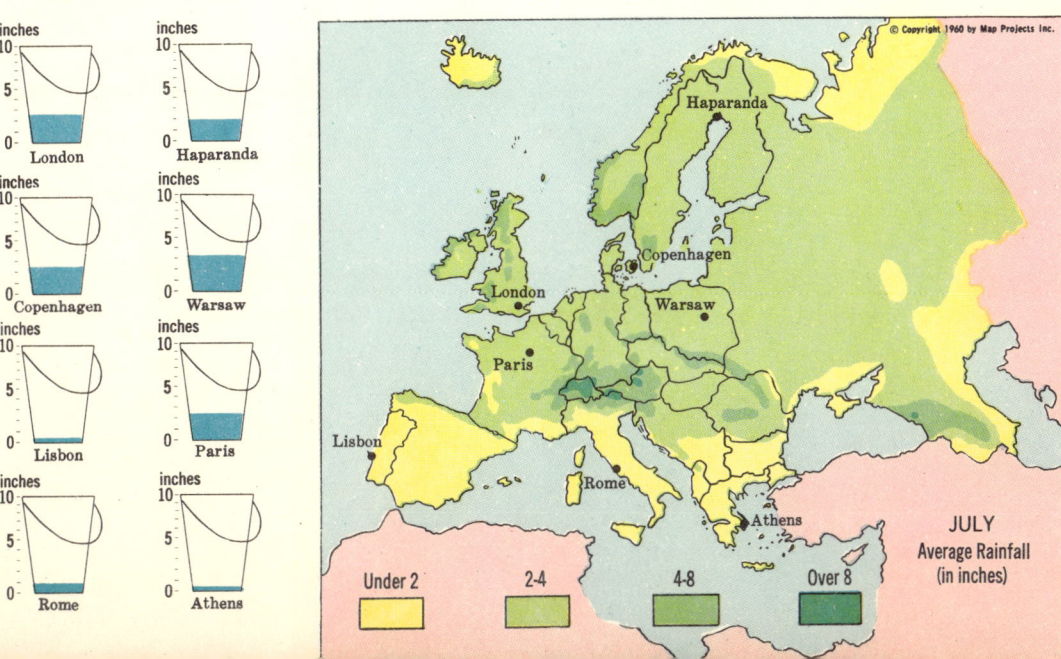

Plaids, kilts, and a piper playing bagpipes are all part of a wedding procession in Scotland.

PEOPLE OF EUROPE

The most ancient peoples in Europe were pushed to the west by invading tribes from the east who usually had a more highly developed civilization and more powerful weapons.

The Celts are an example of such early inhabitants. Their descendants today include the Bretons of Brittany, and the Irish, Welsh, and Scots. The Manx who live on the Isle of Man in the Irish Sea are Celts. So are the Cornish who live in Cornwall, England. These Celtic people all live on islands or peninsulas in Western Europe, where they were forced by stronger tribes from the east.

Each of these groups of Celts had its own language. Some of these languages have disappeared. Others, such as Breton, Welsh, and Gaelic, may still be heard.

The Romans in the days of their power ruled and colonized much of Europe, especially the south and west. Their descendants include the French, Spanish, Portuguese, Italians, and Romanians. All

The mounted guards at Whitehall Palace, London, are one of Britain's colorful, historic sights.

Irish boys stand by donkey carts loaded with peat. Found in bogs, peat is a common fuel in Eire.

EUROPE 203

Children in Iceland. A higher percentage of people can read and write in Iceland than anywhere else.

A Lapp woman, from Europe's far north, treats a reindeer skin before sewing it into boots.

Bicycles are popular transportation in Copenhagen. One of every two Danes owns a bicycle.

German children must study hard. Both East and West Germany place great stress on education.

these people speak languages that originally came from Latin.

In Britain the invading Angles, Saxons, and Danes wiped out almost all trace of the Roman tongue and culture. Similar invasions wiped out Latin in other parts of Europe where Rome had ruled peoples of different languages and cultures.

Many of the "barbarians" that invaded the Roman Empire were of Germanic stock. They are represented today by the English, Dutch, German, and Scandinavian peoples.

After the Germanic invasions, tribes that spoke Slavic languages came from Asia and settled in Eastern Europe. Their descendants are the Russians, Poles, Czechs, Slovaks, Serbs, Croats, Slovenes, and Bulgarians.

Thus we see that today the three great

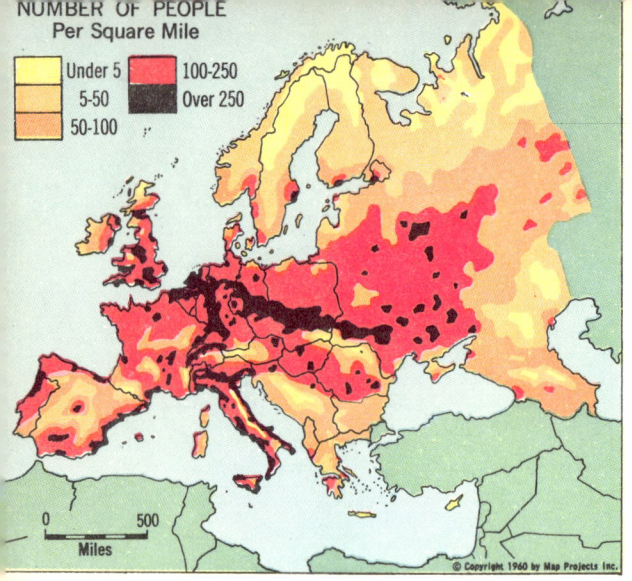

language and cultural groups of Europe are the Romance (derived from Latin), the Germanic, and the Slavic.

The influence of the culture of ancient Rome is still shown in the alphabet we use. All the countries of Western Europe use the same alphabet that the Romans did. When the Slavs invaded Europe, Roman culture had lost much of its influence. But it was still strong enough to give its alphabet to the westernmost Slavs, that is, the Poles, Czechs, and Slovenes.

The tribes of the East, however, did not adopt the Roman alphabet. In the 800's a monk named Cyril invented an alphabet for them. It was based on Greek as well as on Roman letters. This Cyrillic alphabet is the one used today by the Serbs, Croats, Bulgarians, and Russians.

There are also several smaller groups of European peoples. The Greeks long ago drove out or conquered the original inhabitants and settled in Greece. They still live there and on the nearby Aegean Islands. In ancient days far-flung Greek colonies were scattered over the Mediterranean Sea, especially in Sicily and Italy. Indeed, "Naples" comes from two Greek words meaning "New City."

Today there are many descendants of the Greeks scattered from Spain to Istanbul. But the language and way of life of these early Greek settlers have been changed into that of the populations that came after them.

Other smaller groups are the Finns and the Hungarians. The Finns, whose culture now is much like that of the Scandinavians, have a quite different language. It is related to Estonian and to Hungarian. Both of these peoples also have their own language and way of life.

Besides the Hungarians in Hungary, groups of Hungarians are also found in Yugoslavia and in Romania. The Turks, who once conquered European lands as far as Vienna, are now confined to a foothold around Istanbul in southeastern Europe. They have their own language and culture, as have the Albanians, who live in the rugged uplands northwest of Greece.

Most Europeans are white. Many of those that live in the north are tall and have blue eyes and light hair. Those that live in the south tend to be shorter and to have dark eyes and dark hair.

Thousands of years have gone by since the first men came into Europe. In that time tribes have conquered tribes and nations have conquered nations. Victors and vanquished have mingled and married. And the blood of Greek and Roman, Celt, German, and Slav is now widely spread throughout the continent.

Round loaves of bread such as these are sold in open markets on the streets in Spain.

Ewing Krainin—Photo Researchers

TRANSPORTATION

The geographic position of Europe gives it great advantages for overseas transportation and trade. It is close to Africa and Asia Minor. North America, the West Indies, and South America are within easy reach across the ocean.

Europe's irregular coastline, protected seas, wide river mouths, and slow-flowing rivers provide excellent harbors. They also encourage river and coastwise transportation and overseas trade. European merchant marine lines go to all parts of the globe. London, Antwerp, Rotterdam, and Hamburg are among the busiest ports in the world.

Due to the levelness of the central plain, canals have proved a low-cost means of transportation, particularly in Holland, Belgium, Germany, and France.

Western Europe has the densest network of railways in the world. Belgium, for example, has one mile of railway for every four square miles of land. In Eastern Europe railroads are also important, but there are fewer miles of track.

Exceeded only by North America, Western Europe holds second place in the world in the number of automobiles. The superhighways of Germany, built in the 1930's, were the first of the 4-6 lane thruway-type highways in Europe.

Eastern Europe has fewer cars and the roads are not as good. Throughout the continent much use is still made of the horse. Even oxen may sometimes be seen in remote areas.

The bicycle is a favorite method of transportation everywhere. Both bicycles and motorcycles are much more common in Europe than in North America. They are even used in large cities.

A network of airways covers Britain and the continent and extends to all parts of the world. Almost every country has a major airline.

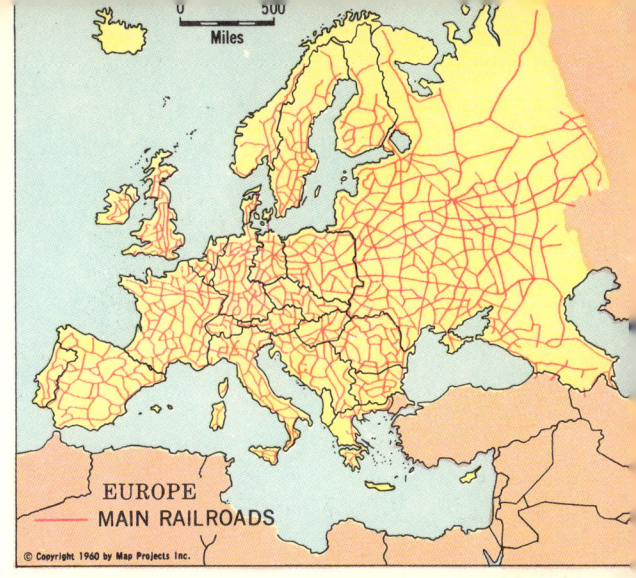

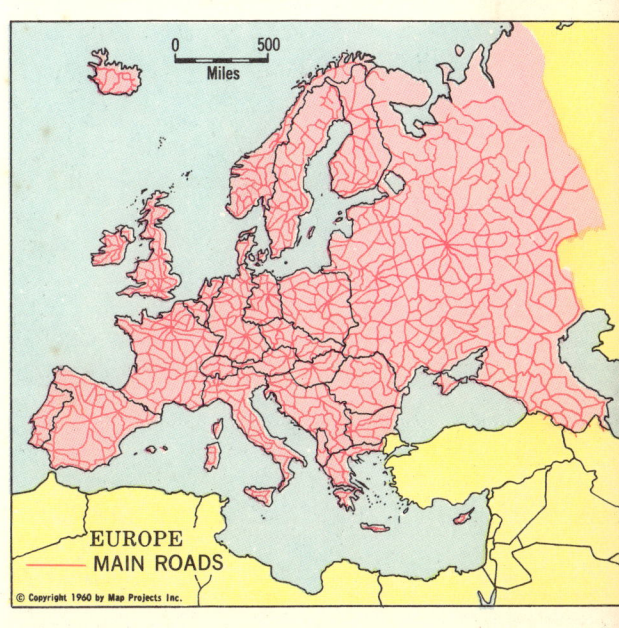

![Westminster Bridge and Big Ben]

Courtesy of TWA—Trans World Airlines
Westminster Bridge and "Big Ben" clock, London

Nôtre Dame, the world-famous cathedral in Paris
Courtesy of TWA—Trans World Airlines

EUROPE'S CITIES

Europe is a continent with many cities. Not counting those in the Soviet Union, 18 cities have a population of more than 1,000,000 and 264 have more than 100,000. London, with over 8,200,000 people, is the second largest in the world. Almost every city—and there are many smaller ones, too—is growing rather fast in size and in population.

Most European cities grew out of medieval villages which first developed as small trading centers. Life there was freer than it was in the countryside where the farm workers were forced by their landlords, who were also their rulers, to remain on the land and to pay many heavy taxes.

Villages gradually grew into towns and towns grew into cities. As these "free cities," as many were called, became larger and stronger, they helped break the power of the ruling landlords. In time the cities became very important in building the foundations of modern commercial and industrial society.

Many cities grew up near the sea as ports of the maritime trading countries. Examples are Glasgow, Liverpool, Hamburg, and Genoa. Others, such as Paris, Vienna, and Warsaw, developed as centers of trade in agricultural regions. These and many other inland cities were located on navigable rivers. Such waterways were natural highways—much easier for travel than muddy roads.

With the development of rail transport, railway centers often became important population centers. And many existing towns became even more important because of railroads. In recent years, nearness to sources of raw materials, coal, water power, or markets has led to the founding or rapid growth of many cities.

European cities as a rule are older—sometimes much older—than those in America. Despite the ravages of war and

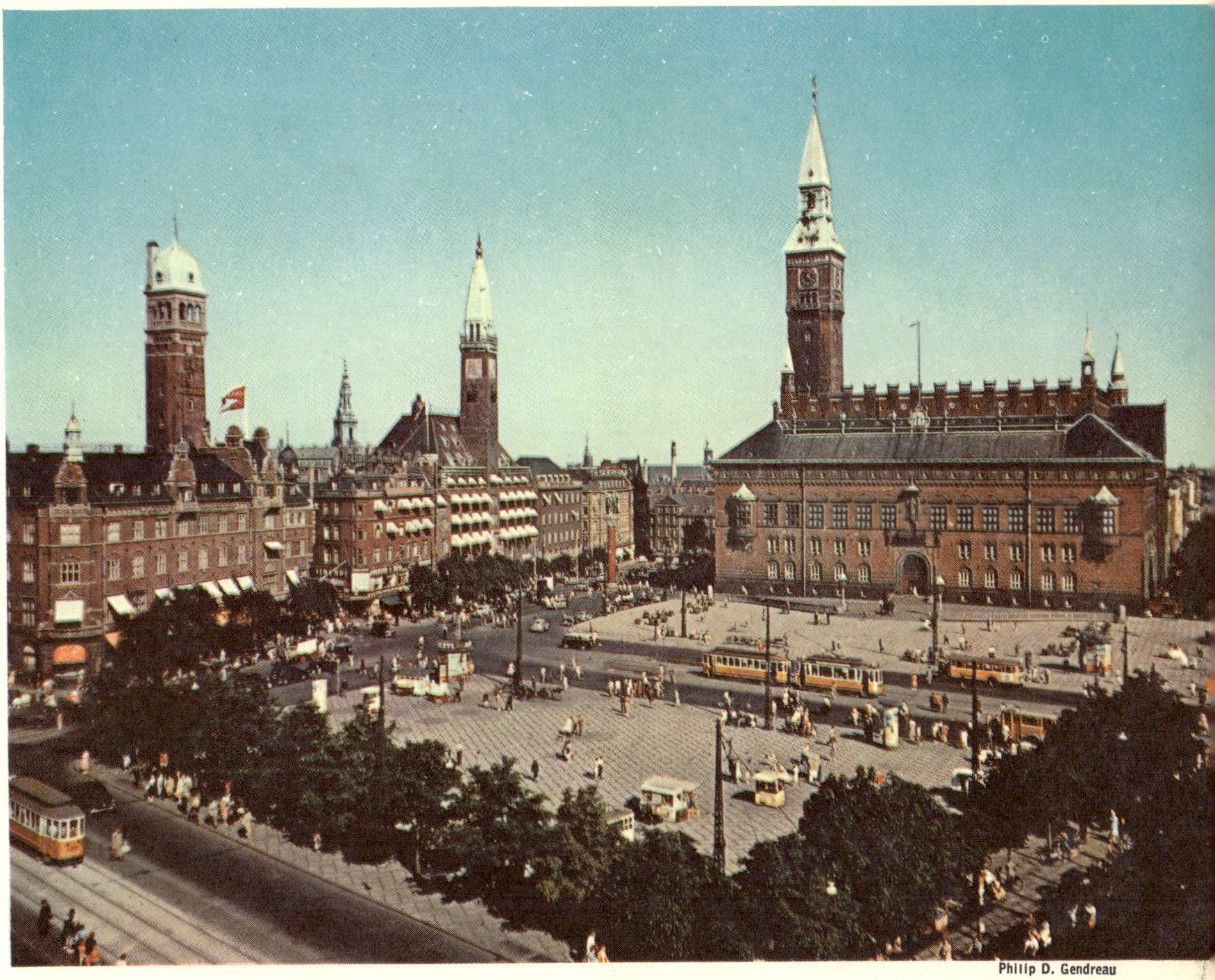

Philip D. Gendreau

The stands on Copenhagen's Town Hall Square sell ice cream, chocolates, and newspapers.

In Amsterdam, the Netherlands' largest city, many buildings date back to the seventeenth century.

Max Tatch—Shostal

Kurfürstendamm is one of the main streets of the western sector of Berlin, Germany.

Tom Hollyman—Photo Researchers

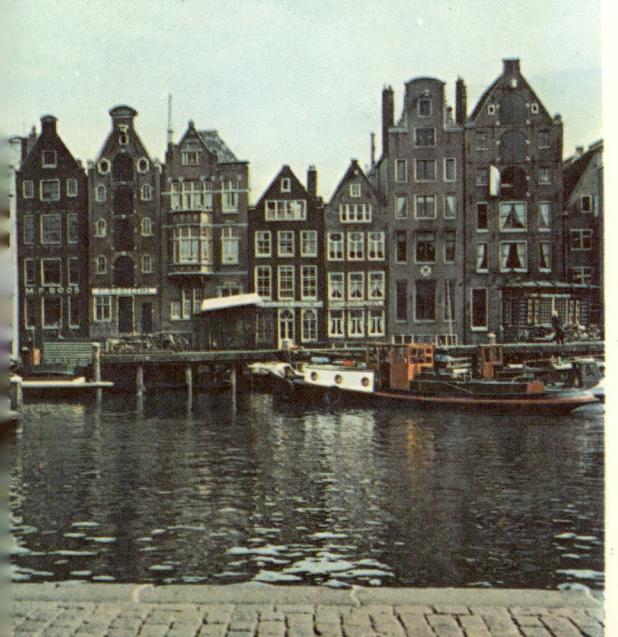

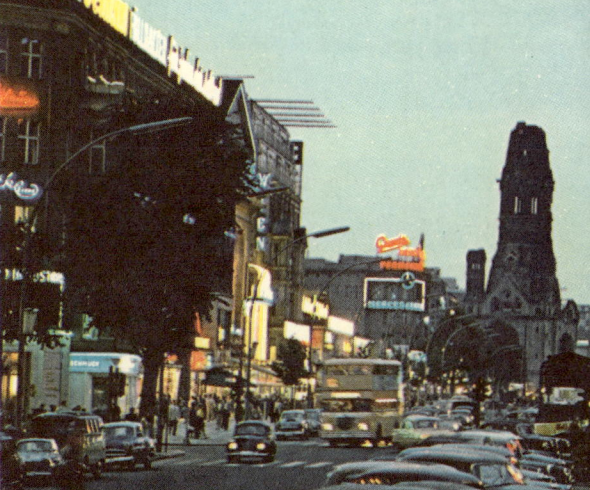

Lisbon, Portugal, with one of the finest harbors in the world, has been a port since Roman times.

the wear and tear of time, many still retain some of their ancient buildings.

Some towns, such as Chester in England, have traces of the walls, gates, and moats of the Middle Ages, when they were fortified for defense against raids by neighboring noblemen. In larger centers, like Paris or Vienna, these have usually been replaced by broad avenues or parkways. But in the middle of a city—London and Istanbul are good examples — we often find narrow, winding streets and historic buildings.

Two hundred years ago the largest cities in Europe were London and Paris. Each had 750,000 people. But with the coming of the Industrial Revolution towns and larger metropolitan centers grew fast, both in number and in size.

Rapid urban growth encouraged some city planning even in the nineteenth century. The broad boulevards of Paris, for example, were among the first laid out in

Madrid is Spain's capital and largest city. It is a center for railroads and airlines.

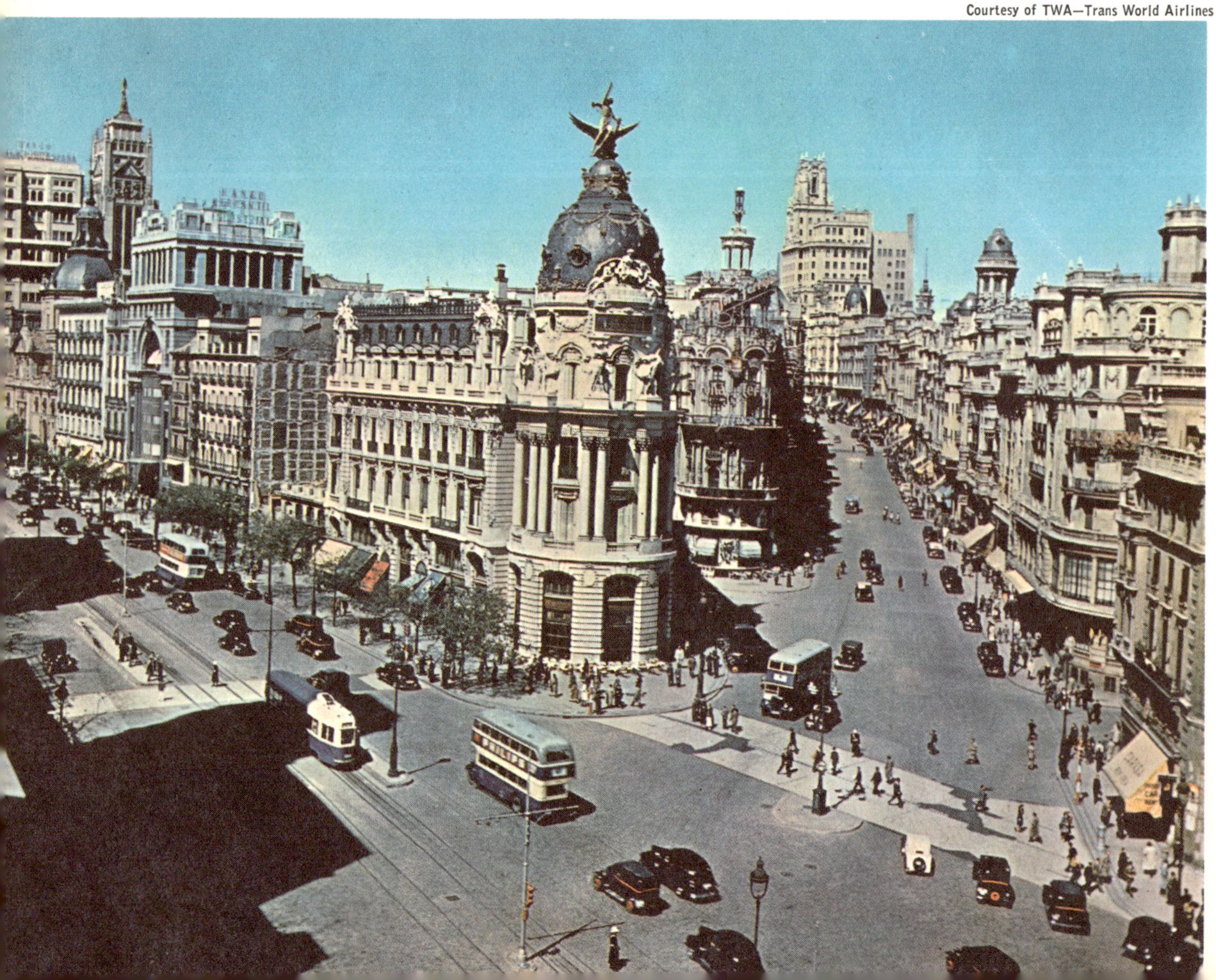

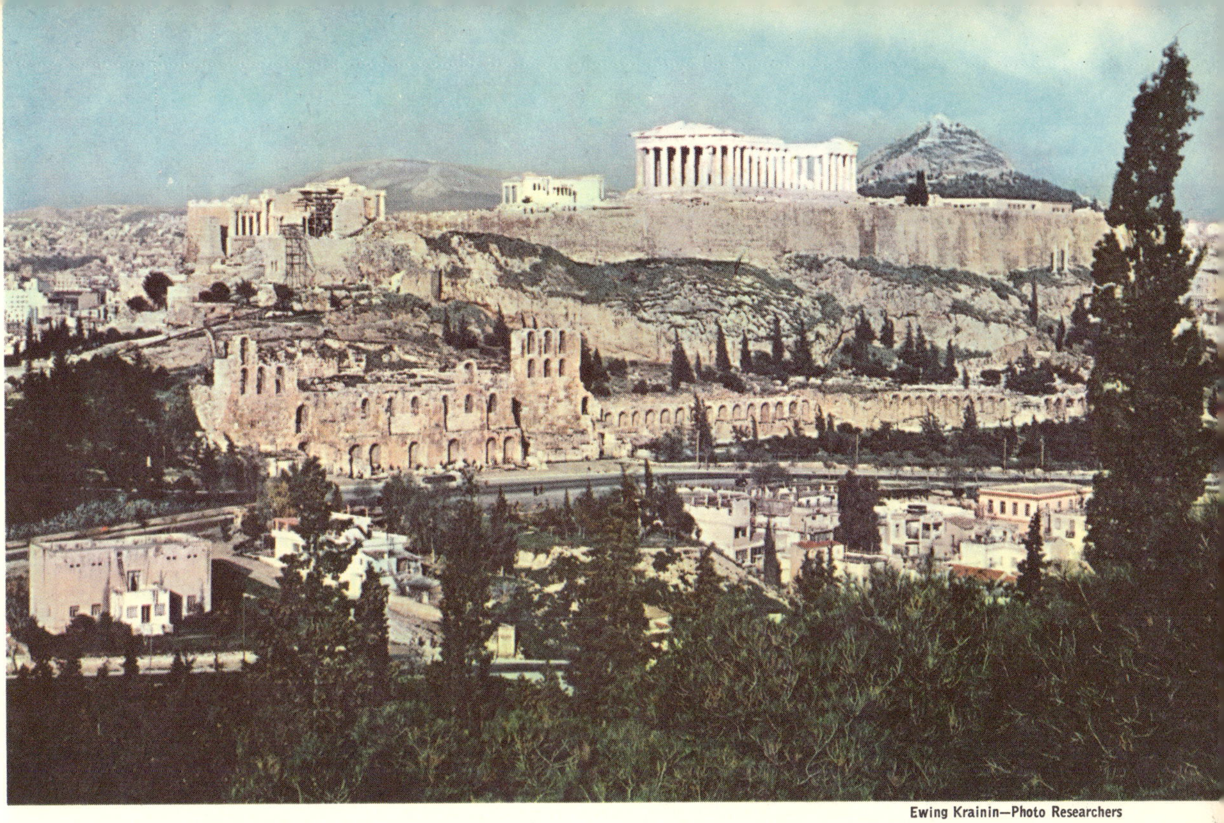

Ewing Krainin—Photo Researchers

The Parthenon symbolizes Greece's past, but Athens is a bustling modern city.

a modern city. Planning for beauty and for the health and comfort of the people has become increasingly important in recent years. This is especially so in the rebuilding of cities damaged or destroyed in World War II.

Some cities still have large slums and poor-looking areas. But in the more up-to-date centers new parks, buildings, and wide avenues show what planning can do to make a modern city beautiful and more pleasant to live in.

Each city has its own character and atmosphere. From one end of Europe to the other they show much greater variety than do those of North America. Rome, for instance, is famous for its beautiful fountains. Paris is known for its flowers and sidewalk cafés.

The capital of each European country almost always is its largest city. Life in it is fairly typical of the nation and people. But for quaint or old-fashioned ways or costumes you must go to outlying districts. The pictures we show illustrate a few of the aspects of life in some of these capitals.

Courtesy of TWA—Trans World Airlines

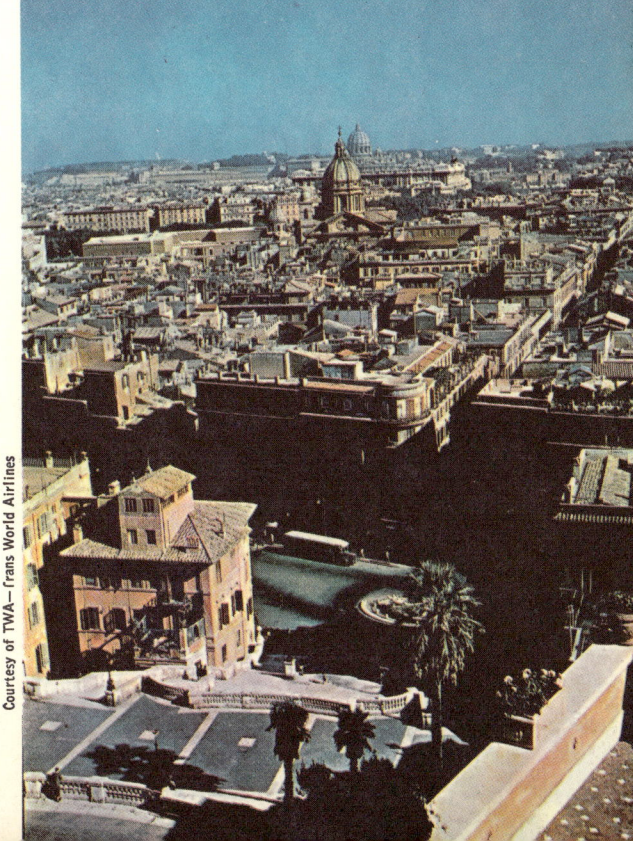

Rome, the capital of Italy, contains Vatican City, center of the Roman Catholic Church.

Joe Barnell—Shostal

St. Stephen's Cathedral towers over Vienna, the capital of Austria. Vienna, the home of Mozart and many other famous composers, is the music center of Europe.

Eleven bridges span the Vltava (Moldau) River in Prague, Czechoslovakia. Once called the "golden city of a hundred spires," historic Prague is a great manufacturing city.

Eastfoto

Many lakes and low islands show that Finland was once covered by a great ice sheet.

NORTHERN EUROPE

Northern Europe consists of Norway, Sweden, Denmark, Finland, and Iceland. Norway and Sweden occupy the Scandinavian peninsula. Norway, Sweden, and Denmark are sometimes called the Scandinavian countries. Iceland is an island in the North Atlantic. Norway, Finland, and Denmark each have about 4,000,000 people. Sweden has more than 7,000,000. Iceland has only 160,000.

The Scandinavian peninsula has a backbone of mountains, running northeast and southwest. To the south and east the land is lower. Denmark and the southern parts of Sweden and Finland are rather flat. Iceland is rugged.

Northern Europe reaches further north than Labrador. But the warm waters of the Gulf Stream that flow northeast past Iceland and around the west coast of Norway give it a rather moderate climate.

Northern Norway, Sweden, and Finland are north of the Arctic Circle. This is the Land of the Midnight Sun. There, in the far north, from May to July the sun never sets.

A few thousand years ago Northern Europe was covered with a great ice sheet. This scooped out hollows on the lowlands, while glaciers carved U-shaped valleys in the sides of the mountains. When the ice melted, the hollows became lakes. The

Icelandic women cleaning herring. Fishing is an important source of income for Iceland.

Patrick Morin—Monkmeyer

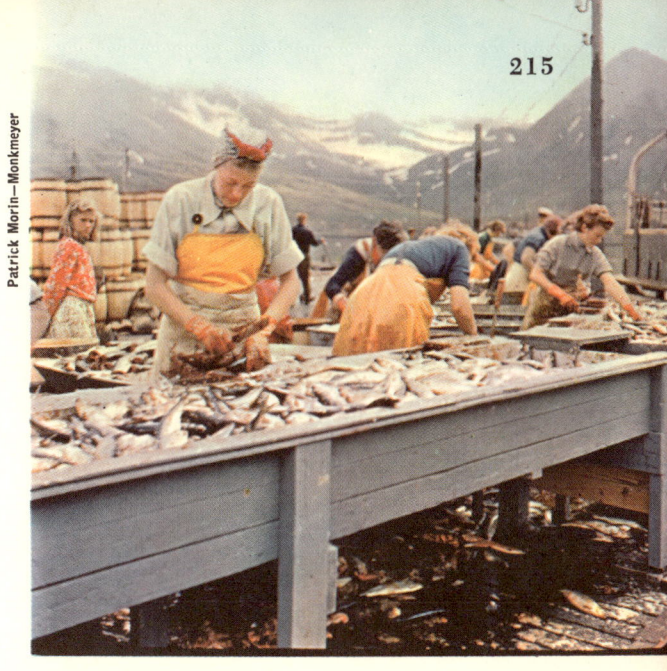

sea rose, flooded the U-shaped valleys, and made them into fiords. These are narrow arms of the sea with steep mountain sides. In the mountains and in Iceland there are still some glaciers. Iceland also has active volcanoes and hot springs.

After the European ice sheet melted, forests covered the land. Fur-clad hunters and fishermen followed. They lived off deer and reindeer in the forests, off fish and shellfish along the seashore. Living close to salt water, they became great boatbuilders and sailors. The Vikings, as they came to be known about A.D. 700, attacked England, settled Iceland and Greenland, and may have discovered North America before Columbus. Finally they settled down into the nations we know today.

The Norwegians, Swedes, Danes, and Icelanders have separate but similar languages, related to German and English. The languages of the Finns and of the wandering tribes of Lapps are different.

Norwegian children dressed in gay costumes do a folk dance in a meadow near Hardanger Fiord.
Roy Pinney—Photo Library

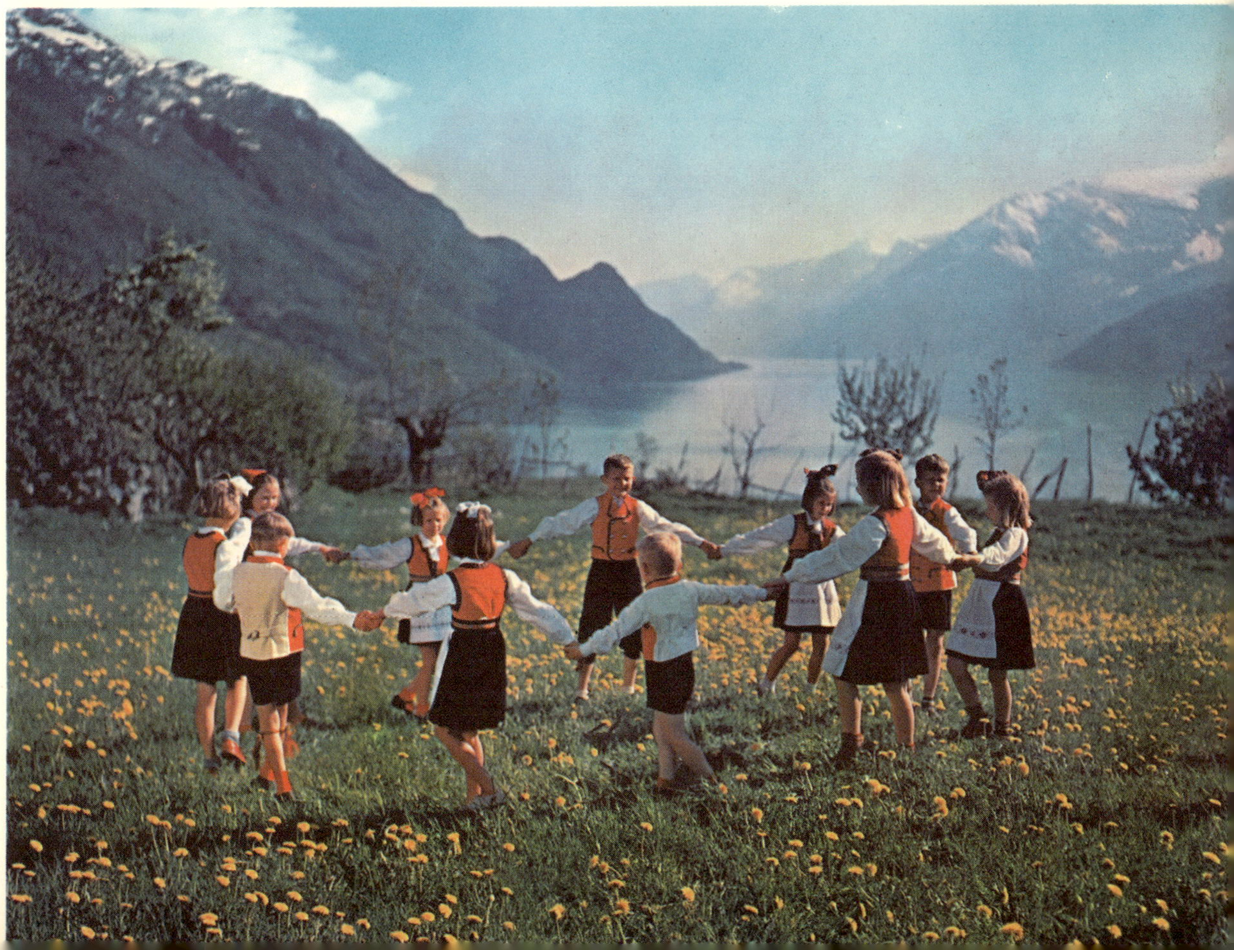

Fishing and Forestry

Fishing is an important source of wealth for all the countries of Northern Europe except Finland. Indeed, fish are the chief resource of Iceland. The Scandinavians catch their fish in the North and Baltic seas and in the North Atlantic Ocean. Icelanders fish in the waters around Iceland. Herring, cod, mackerel, halibut, and haddock are the chief species taken.

Fishing "grounds" or "banks" are what fishermen call parts of the sea where fish are common. They are usually rather shallow. The North Sea is one of the richest fishing grounds in the world. The Grand Banks off Newfoundland are other rich fishing grounds.

In addition to the salt-water species mentioned Swedes also catch pike, perch, trout, and salmon. These are fresh-water species. They are caught in Sweden's many lakes and rivers. Salt-water fishing in Sweden is centered around the port of Göteborg. Danish commercial fishing also includes oysters, shrimp, and eels. Refrigerated trucks take Danish fish to markets in nearby countries.

Norwegians are the world's greatest whalers. They send more ships to the Antarctic and catch more whales there each year than any other country. Norway is the headquarters of the International Whaling Commission. This Commission keeps statistics on whaling and enforces the international agreements that limit the number of whales that can be killed.

Finland is the most important country in Northern Europe for its wood products. Forests cover three quarters of the land. Finns are expert lumbermen. Finland's lakes and waterways provide an easy means of transportation for logs.

In most forests a forester marks each tree that is to be cut. Loggers, or lumberjacks, cut down the marked trees in winter. At one time oxen or horses then

Sharp-eyed Danish customers inspect the eels of the women fish-vendors in Copenhagen.

Norwegian fishermen pull in a net full of cod. Fishing is Norway's principal industry.

Patrick Morin—Monkmeyer

Old-time whalers killed off almost all Atlantic whales. But Icelanders still catch a few.

Wolfe Worldwide Films, Los Angeles 24, Calif.

Stockholm, Sweden, is built on islands. Men fish with these round nets even in the heart of the city.

hauled the logs on sledges over the snow to the bank of a lake or river. Now tractors do most of the hauling. When spring melts the ice, the lumberjacks float the logs downstream to the mills.

The mountains and foothills of Norway and Sweden are covered with forests that produce much timber. The governments in these countries own one quarter of their woodlands. In both public and private forests North Europeans use modern conservation methods in order to keep up a steady supply of lumber year after year.

Iceland has few original woodlands but is trying to overcome this shortage with an active tree planting program.

Finnish lumbermen collect logs on Lake Päijänne. Pine, spruce, and fir are Finland's "green gold."

Joe Barnell—Shostal

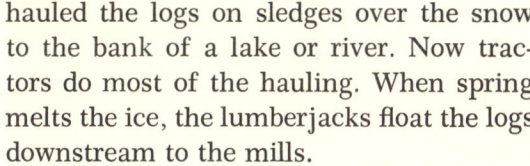

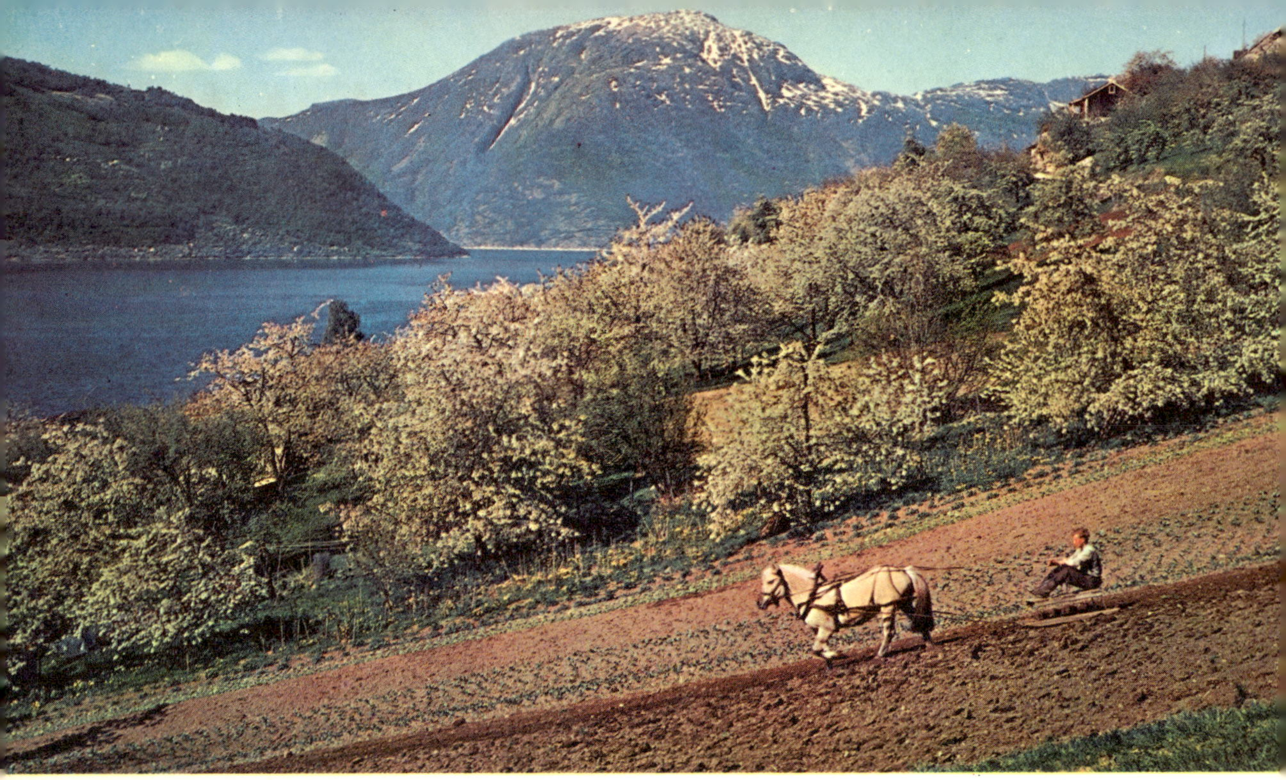

Roy Pinney—Photo Library

A farmer plows a hillside in rugged Norway. Hillside farming often encourages erosion.

Danish cheeses, like these being cured in a warehouse, are eaten all over the world.

Turck—Shostal

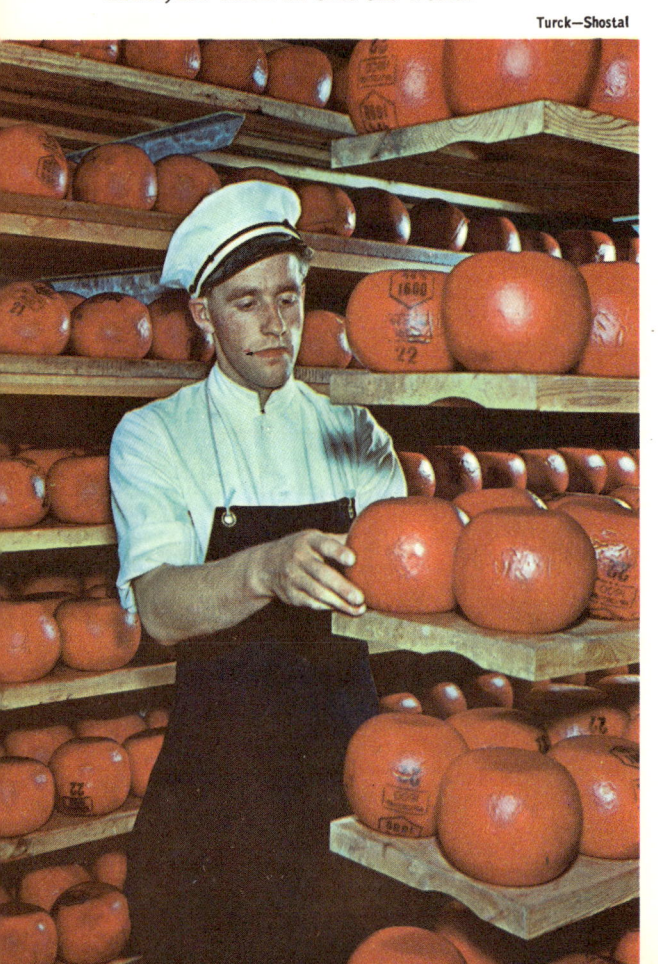

Agriculture

Northern Europe is a land of small farms. In all countries but Iceland one quarter or more of the people make their living from agriculture. In Iceland farms are fewer and larger.

On the mountain pastures of Norway and Iceland cattle, sheep, goats, and ponies graze in summer. Norway is noted for its goat's milk cheese. In Sweden cattle and hogs are raised chiefly in the low country in the southeast.

Denmark is famous for its cows and hogs. Danish butter and cheese, ham, and bacon are world-renowned. In Lapland the people depend upon reindeer for food, skins, and transportation.

Farmers in Norway's narrow valleys grow oats, potatoes, and rye. They harvest hay from hillside pastures. In addition to these crops, the Swedes, Finns, and Danes also raise much wheat and barley. Finnish farmers often grow timber.

On flat lands in Sweden and Denmark much modern farm machinery is used.

NORTHERN EUROPE

Farmers in both these countries pride themselves on their advanced methods of agriculture. Swedish farm boys and girls are organized into farm improvement societies like our own 4-H clubs.

The Icelandic summer is too short to grow anything but hay and potatoes. But in greenhouses warmed by hot springs, grapes, tomatoes, and even bananas are grown!

Denmark is noted for its farm cooperatives. Groups of farmers join together to market their products jointly in order to save money. These cooperatives also buy expensive farm machinery which no one could have afforded to buy alone.

Consumers also join in cooperatives. These cooperatives buy goods at wholesale prices and sell them to their members at a saving. Both producer and consumer cooperatives are an important part of the business life in northern Europe.

Joe Barnell—Shostal

Cows are milked on a Finnish dairy farm. Over half the population is engaged in agriculture.

This Swedish farmer can harvest his wheat by machine because his land is level.

David Forbert—Shostal

Swedish National Travel Office

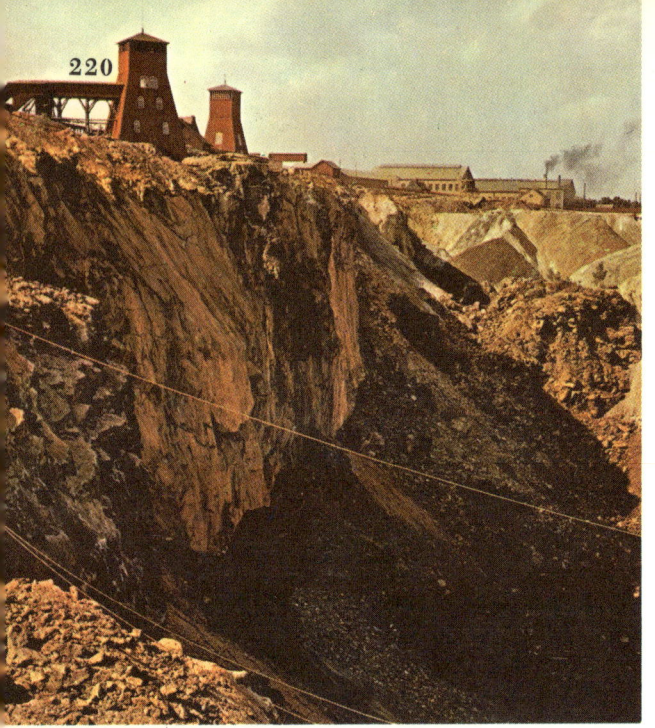

Falun, in north central Sweden, has one of the world's oldest copper mines, dating from 1230.

Mining and Industry

Sweden is the fourth-largest producer of iron ore in the world. Its great mines at Kiruna yield a very high-grade ore. Other ores, such as sulfur, zinc, copper, and manganese, are mined in central Sweden. Norway has iron mines in the north and obtains coal from its arctic island of Spitsbergen. However, water power remains the chief source of energy in Norway and Sweden.

Norway recently built a big iron and steel works at Mo, in the far north. Norway and Sweden have important industries in machine tools, metals, chemicals, aluminum, and textiles. Sweden has long been famous for ball bearings and matches.

The great forests of Norway, Sweden, and Finland have encouraged the production of lumber, furniture, pulp, cellulose, paper, and other wood products. Sweden and Finland both export much paper to

Göteborg, Sweden's chief port, is a shipbuilding and manufacturing center.

Roy Pinney—Photo Library

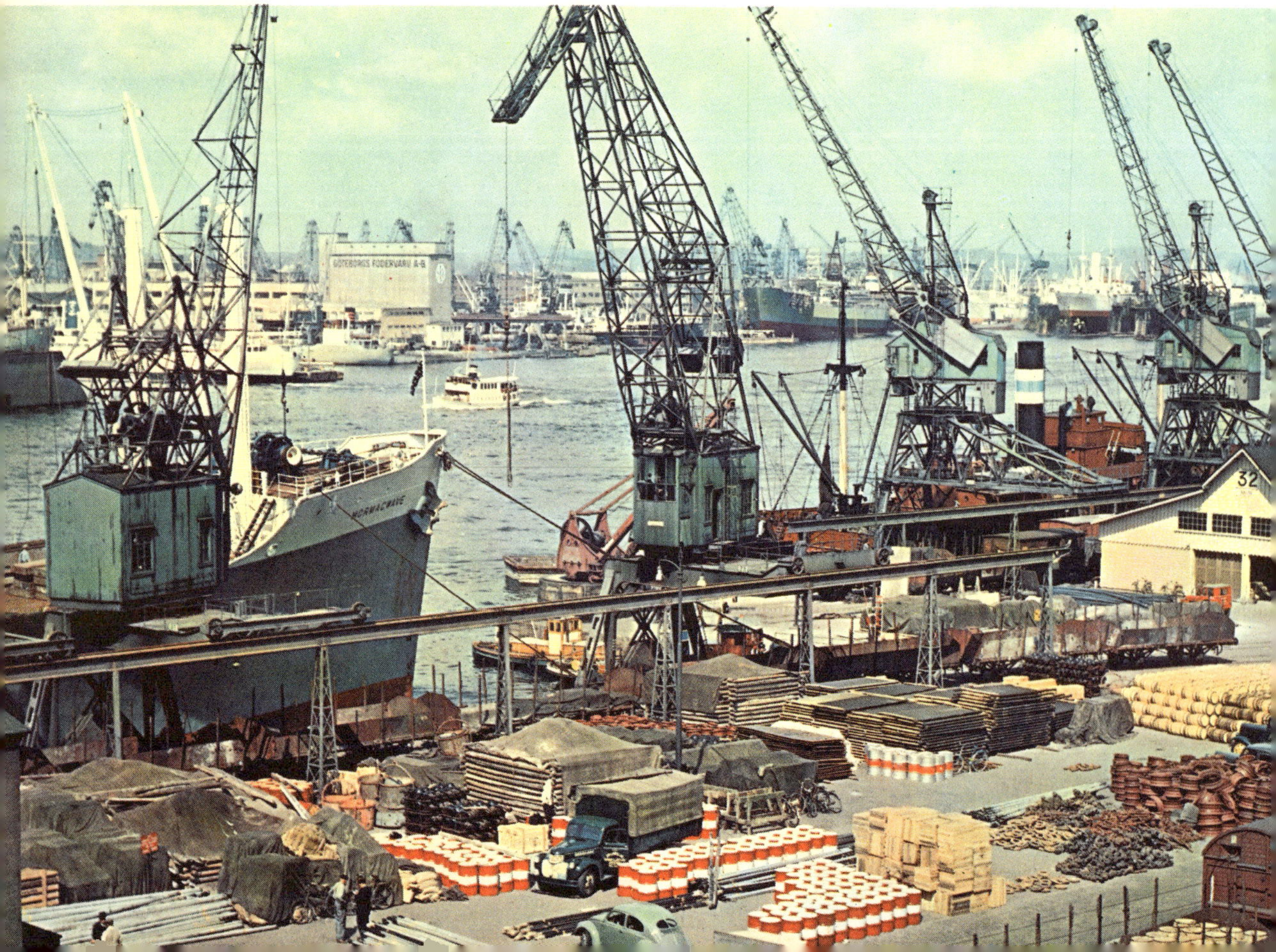

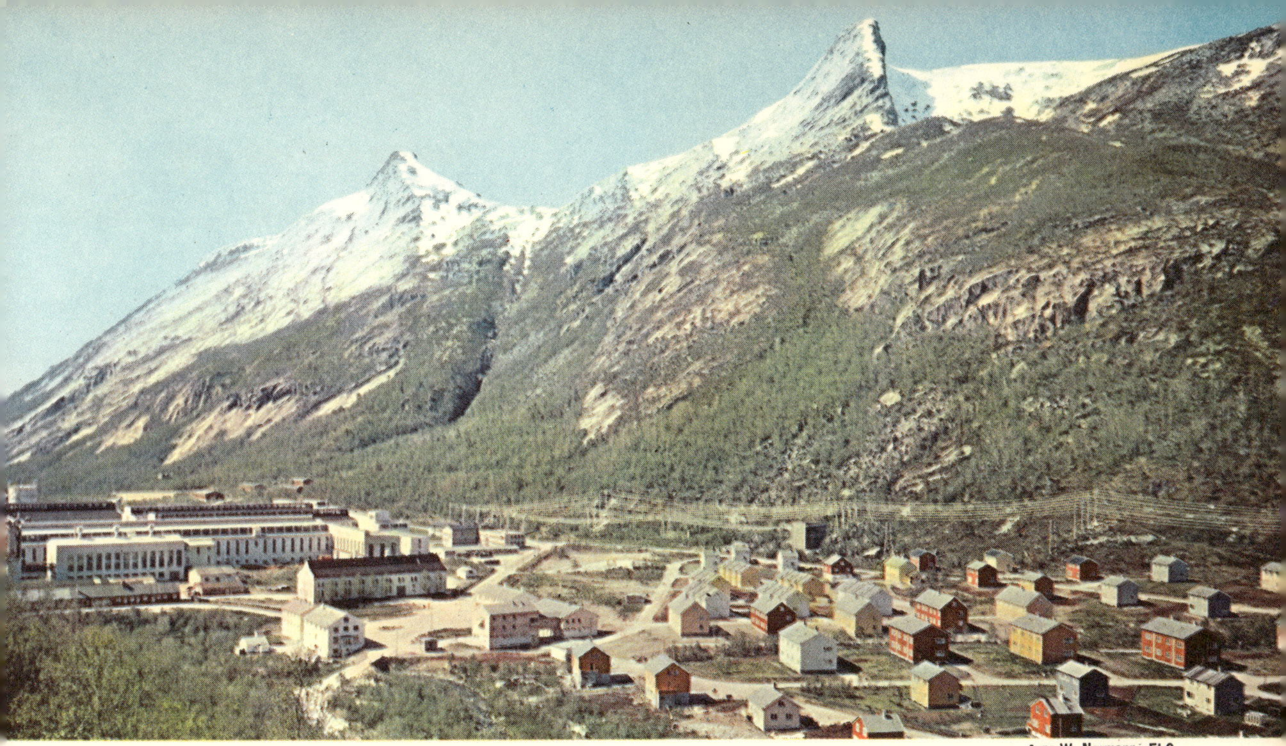

Arne W. Normann—FLO

Hydroelectric plants turn Scandinavia's mountain streams into power for homes and factories.

the United States. Finland is also noted for her plywood. Plywood is made of thin sheets of wood glued together crosswise and is stronger than ordinary wood of the same thickness.

Being so close to salt water and having iron and wood near at hand, all the countries of Northern Europe have important shipbuilding industries. Sweden is the most highly industrialized of these countries. Seven out of ten people live in cities. Two out of every five Swedes are engaged in manufacturing.

In Denmark half the people live in cities. One out of every three persons makes his living from industry. The Danes specialize in Diesel engines, electrical equipment, and bicycles.

Danish manufactures also include food processing, such as the making of margarine and the canning and drying of milk. Creameries scattered over Denmark help supply much of Western Europe with butter. And its meat-packing plants are famous for their bacon. In Norway, Sweden, and Denmark many fish are canned. Iceland also cans fish, makes clothing, and prints more books in proportion to her population than any other country.

David Forbert—Shostal

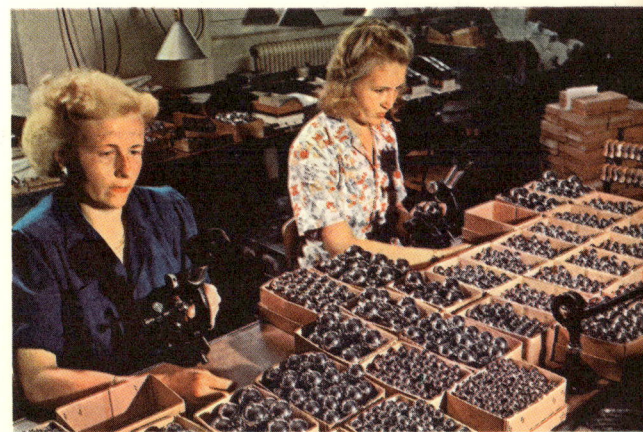

Swedish ball bearings and other precision machinery and tools are known the world over.

Resource-poor Denmark depends on the skill of expert craftsmen like these silversmiths.

David Forbert—Shostal

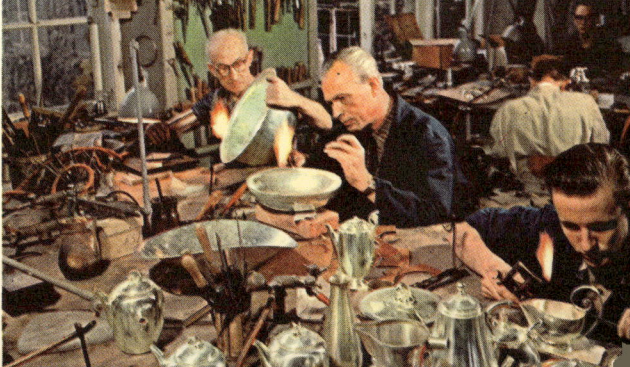

WESTERN EUROPE

Western Europe consists of the British Isles, France, Germany, Switzerland, and Austria. It also includes Belgium, the Netherlands (Holland), and Luxembourg. These three form an economic union called "Benelux." Western Europe includes the most industrialized and heavily populated countries in Europe.

The countries of Western Europe have long been leaders in art and science. The Industrial Revolution (the change from small-scale to large-scale production and the use of machinery instead of man's muscles for power) which began here, made them great and wealthy. Most of them acquired colonies and possessions overseas. By 1914 they almost completely ruled Africa and southern Asia. Today many of the colonies are independent or self-governing. But the mother countries are still powerful in industry and trade.

Much of Western Europe is level or rolling, fertile land. This is true of almost all of Eire, England, Belgium, and Holland, and of much of France and Germany. Across this region flow slow, winding rivers, well suited to navigation, and easy to bridge.

In the Netherlands much of the land was once under water. Netherlanders have built great dikes along the North Sea, drained the water out from behind these dikes, and made fertile fields from this drained land. One of the Netherlands' greatest projects was draining the Zuyder Zee. This large salt-water bay has now been changed into the much smaller freshwater Lake Ijssel. Projects for reclaiming more land are under way.

The highest mountains in Western Europe are the Alps. They extend through all of Switzerland, most of Austria, and parts of southern Germany, southeastern France, and northern Italy. The Alps are young mountains, with steep slopes and sharp, lofty peaks, such as the Matterhorn.

Tom Hollyman—Photo Researchers

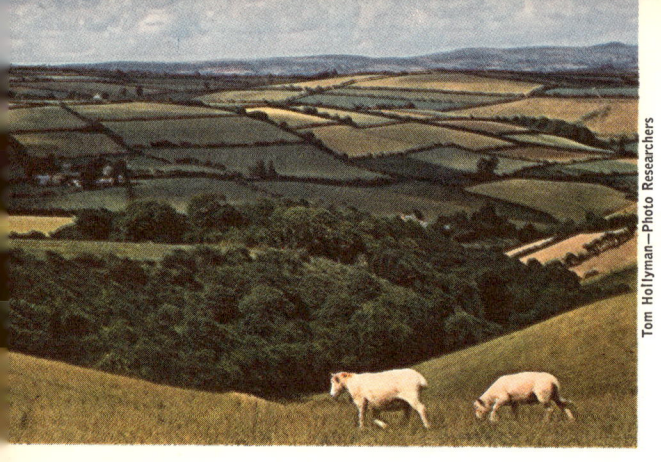

A checkerboard of small fields covers the countryside of Cornwall, in southwest England.

Scotland and Wales are also rugged countries, but their mountains are older and lower. They have rounded summits and gentler slopes. Other mountainous areas in Western Europe are the Central Massif, the Vosges, and the Pyrenees in France, and the Black Forest in Germany.

Streams flowing from the mountains, particularly the Alps and Pyrenees, are used to produce water power. Upland slopes are good for grazing. Sheep and wool and cattle and dairy products are typical of these uplands.

The British Isles geologically are part of Europe and were joined to it until a few thousand years ago. In the Ice Age the ice sheet came down to the Thames Valley in England. It also covered half of the Netherlands and the northern part of Germany. The Alps and Pyrenees were also covered with ice, which spread out over the surrounding foothills.

When the ice melted, a great deal of water was released. The sea rose. This helped cut the English Channel and make the North Sea. The rising sea also flooded,

Scotland's cool climate, short growing season, and poor soil make dairying more important than farming.

Duncan Edwards—FPG

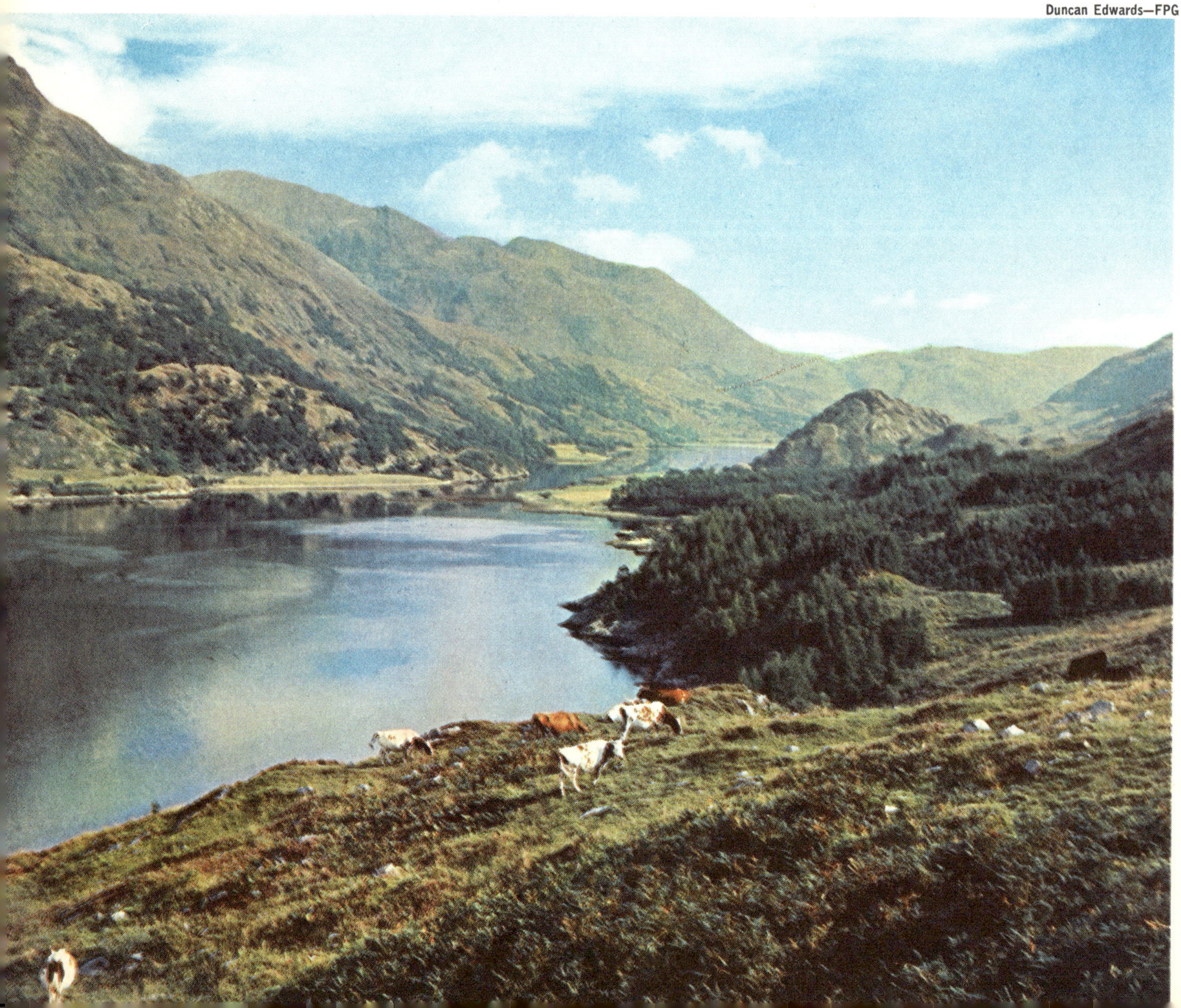

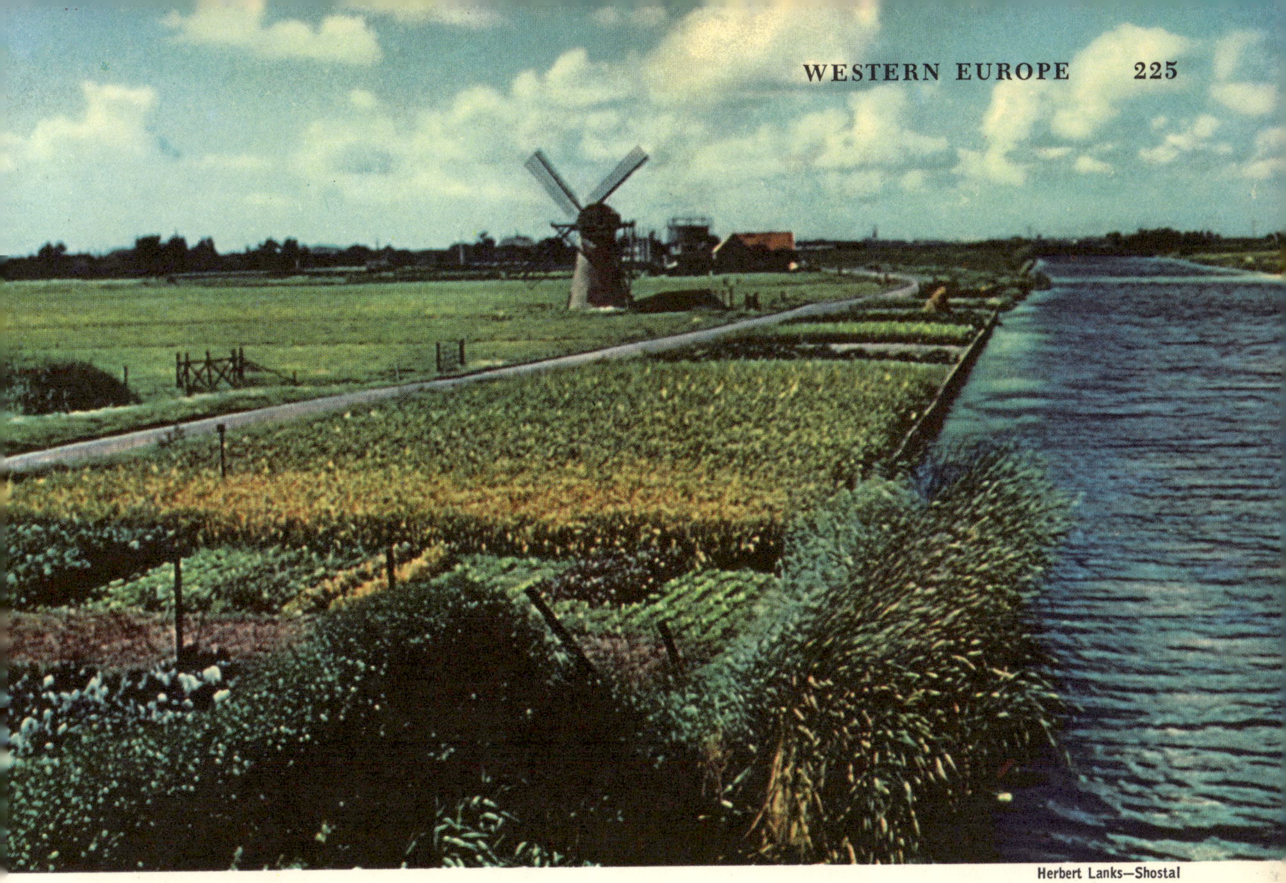

Herbert Lanks—Shostal

Dutch windmills are being replaced by steam and electric power, but about 1,000 remain.

or drowned, the lower valleys of the Rhine, the Seine, and other rivers in Western Europe. These drowned valleys provide good harbors and have thus helped in the development of maritime trade.

Fishing is an important industry along all Western European coasts. British fishermen bring in 1,000,000 tons of fish each year, much of it from the shallow Dogger Bank in the North Sea.

French fishermen along the Bay of Biscay fish for herring and other salt-water species. French fishing boats today travel as far as the Grand Banks off Newfoundland. France uses the little islands of St. Pierre and Miquelon ten miles south of Newfoundland as a North American base for her fishing fleet.

Ostend is the great Belgian fishing port. Many of the 3,000 Dutch fishing boats put out along the canal between Amsterdam and the North Sea. The Germans fish in the North Sea and the Baltic.

Herring and cod are the chief species caught, but some haddock, halibut, tuna, mackerel, and plaice are also taken. The coastal waters of France, Belgium, and the Netherlands produce many oysters.

Splendid hotels line the waterfront of Nice, a winter resort on the sunny French Riviera.

Courtesy of TWA—Trans World Airlines

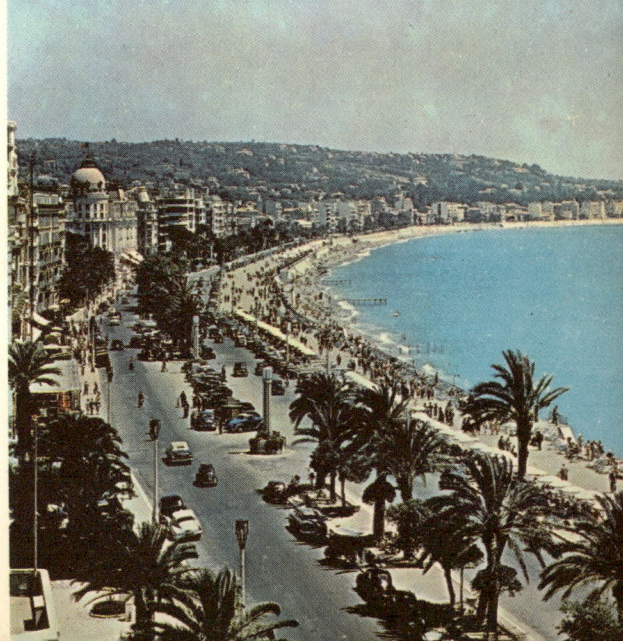

Jerry Cooke—Photo Researchers

These checkered fields are part of the fertile Alsatian plain, located along the Rhine River in France.

Castles along the Rhine were once the strongholds of robber barons who levied tolls on river traffic.

Courtesy of TWA—Trans World Airlines

WESTERN EUROPE 227

Great Britain includes England, Scotland, Wales, and Northern Ireland. It is one of the greatest industrial countries in the world. For two centuries Britain was the leading world power.

Two world wars used up much of Britain's wealth. The United States and the Soviet Union have forged ahead of it as industrial powers. Many of its possessions, notably India, have won independence or been given self-government. But Britain is still a great and thriving power.

Eire occupies the southern four fifths of Ireland. It is largely an agricultural country. After long rule by England it gained complete independence in 1949. But its economy is not highly developed.

France was long the strongest continental power. It is noted for its art, culture, wines, science, and way of life. Three wars with Germany in 75 years have cost it heavily, although in the last two it was among the victors. Recent warfare in Algeria has also cut into its wealth.

Despite all this France has recovered well from World War II. Its economy is strong. And many tourists come each year to see its ancient courts and castles.

The pine-covered Black Forest is located in southwestern Germany. Cuckoo clocks and toys are made here.
Wolff and Tritschler

Belgium is noted for its dense population and industry, and as the battleground of two world wars. The Netherlands is a leading trading nation and also has a great deal of modern industry. Tiny Luxembourg is noted for its iron and steel mills.

Germany is one of the great industrial countries of the world. It is divided into the Federal Republic of Germany (West Germany) and the German Democratic Republic (East Germany). Most World War II damage has now been repaired. West Germany is again a leading industrial nation. In East Germany recovery has not been as spectacular.

Switzerland stayed out of both great wars. It has become an important banking and vacation center. Austria, made poor by defeat in two world wars, is still noted for music and for the great cultural city of Vienna. The Alps in both countries attract thousands of tourists.

Western Europe also has three tiny states. Andorra is an ancient republic high in the Pyrenees. Monaco, on the Mediterranean in southern France, is half the size of New York City's Central Park. Here is the world-famous gambling casino of Monte Carlo. In Liechtenstein, a tiny principality between Switzerland and Austria, many corporations have made their headquarters because taxes are low. Much of its income comes from the sale of postage stamps to collectors.

Glaciers formed the deep valleys of the Swiss Alps, with their "bridal veil" waterfalls.

Courtesy of TWA—Trans World Airlines

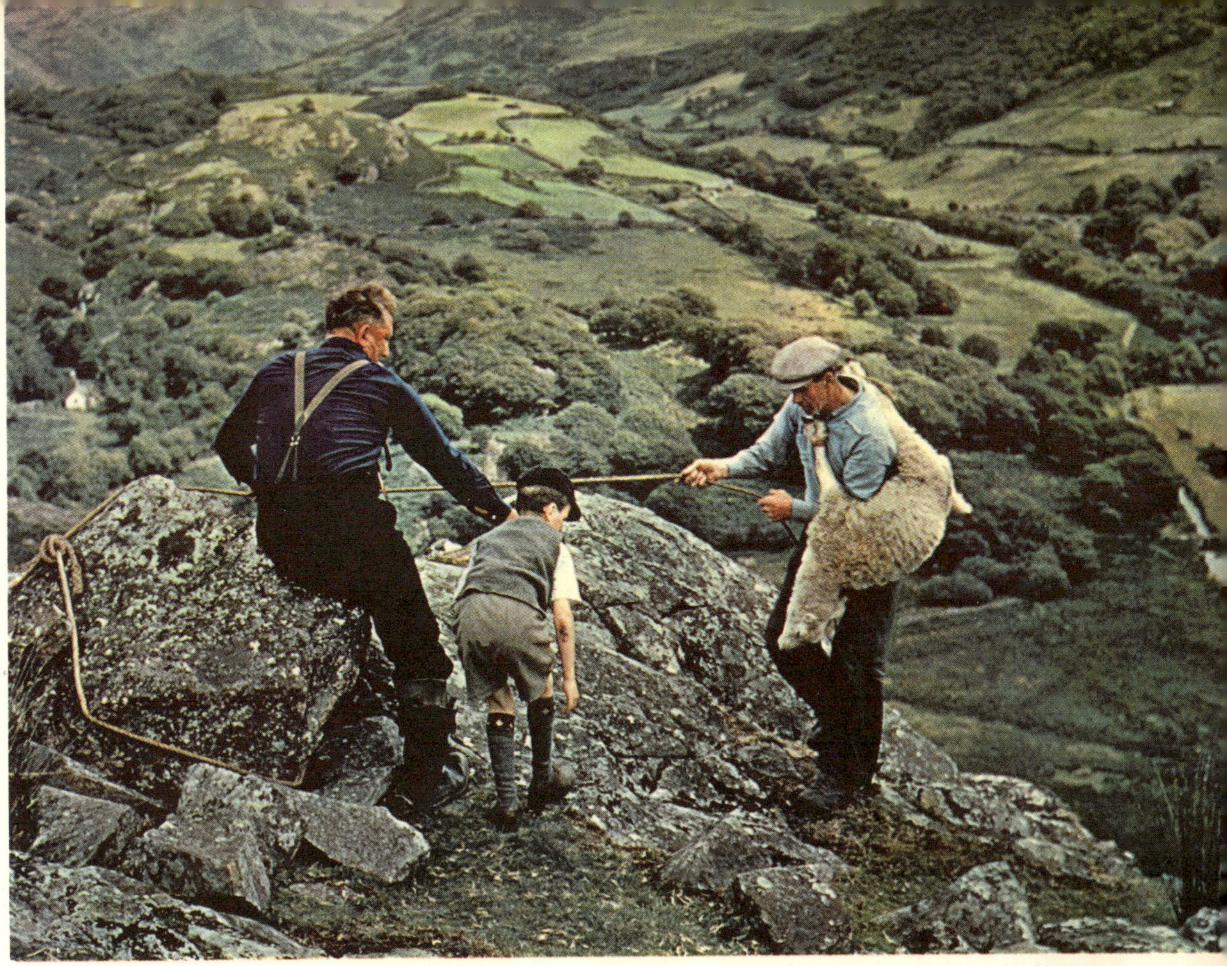

John Hardman

The rough countryside of Wales is good for sheep raising. These men have just found a stray.

Agriculture

Crops in Western Europe, as everywhere, depend upon the altitude, soil, climate, and temperature. To the north and at higher elevations, only those crops that can endure cold and that ripen quickly are successful. On high mountain slopes or where there is too much rain, grains give way to grass and moorlands.

In the fertile central plain wheat, barley, rye, oats, potatoes, sugar beets, and fruit are widely grown. Of these, oats and potatoes will thrive in areas too cold or moist for wheat. Hence, oatmeal is a favorite cereal in Scotland, and we often think of potatoes and Ireland together.

David Forbert—Shostal

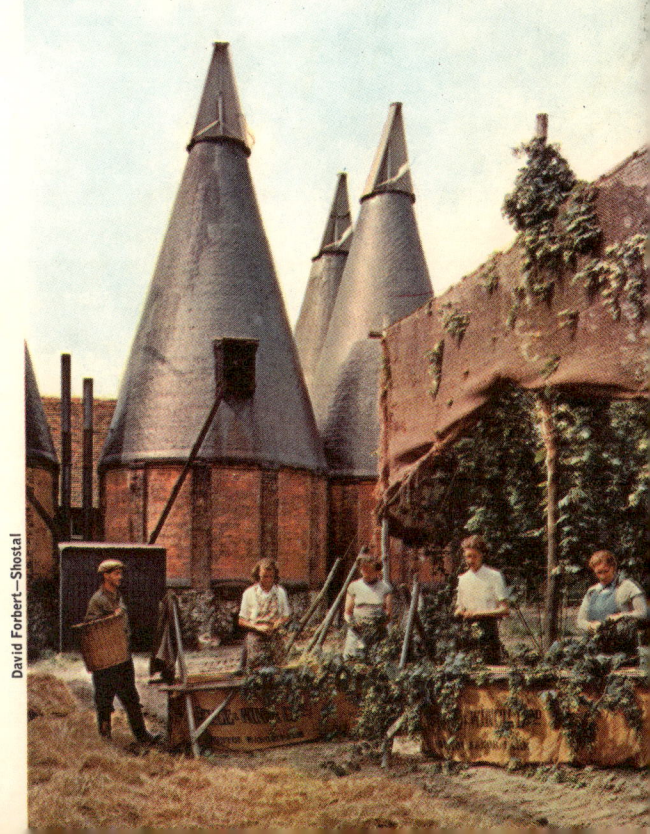

Hops are grown in Kent in southeastern England. These women strip them off the vines.

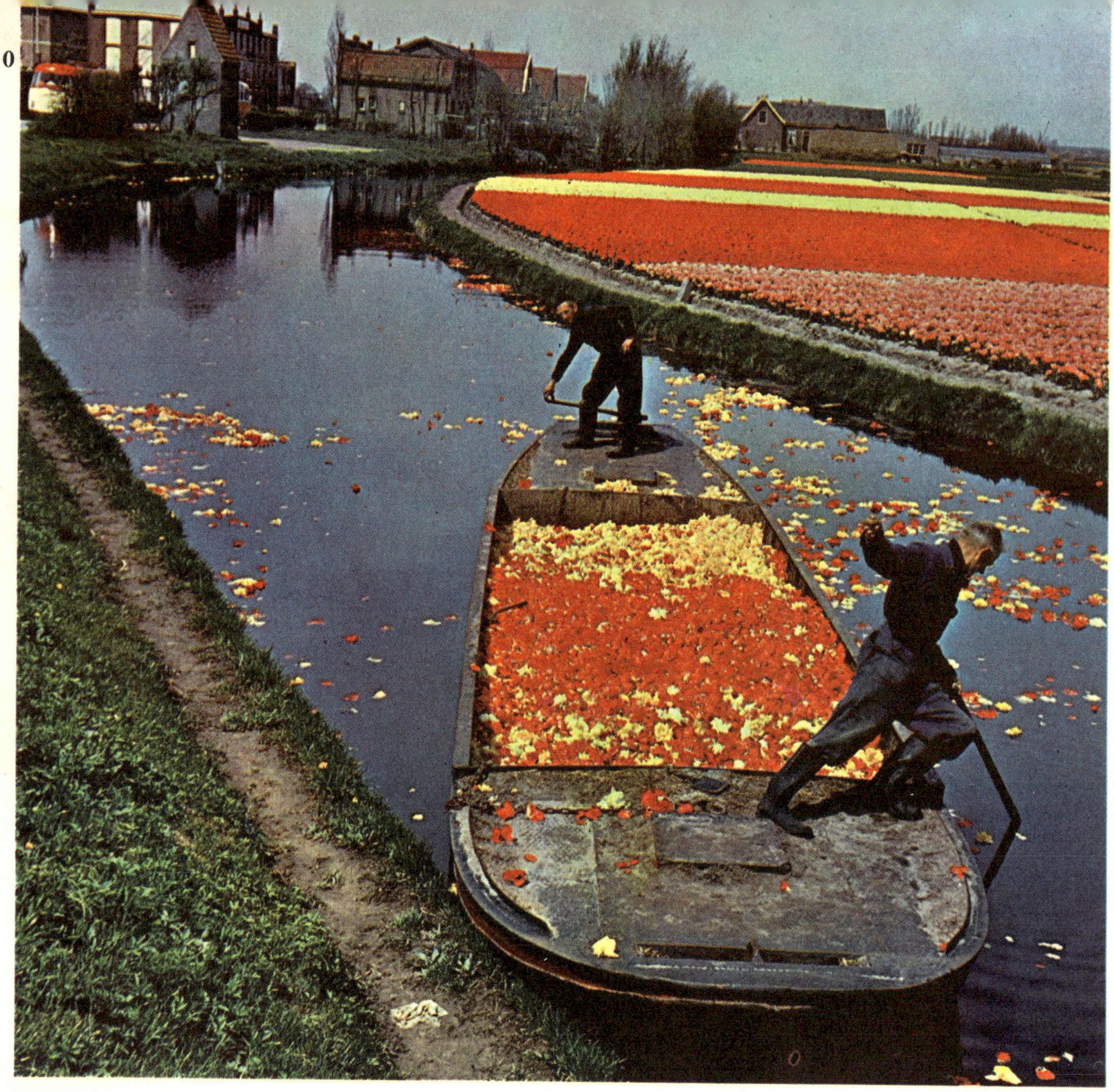

Malak—Annan Photo Features

Bargemen pole a flower-filled barge along a Dutch canal beside fields of growing flowers.

Moisture makes for good grass and grazing. That is why Ireland is called the "Emerald Isle." Everything is so green. As a result Eire raises fine horses and cattle, as well as many pigs and sheep. Moisture also helps in the production of flax, a popular Irish crop and the source of fine Irish linens. Three out of four persons in Eire live off the land.

In Great Britain the opposite is the case. Only one person out of twenty is a farmer or herdsman. But much of the land is agricultural and modern farming methods are widely used.

Wales, Scotland, Northern Ireland, and western England have considerable grazing. Sheep are a British specialty and several sheep breeds are named after English counties. Southeastern England

Jerry Cooke—Photo Researchers

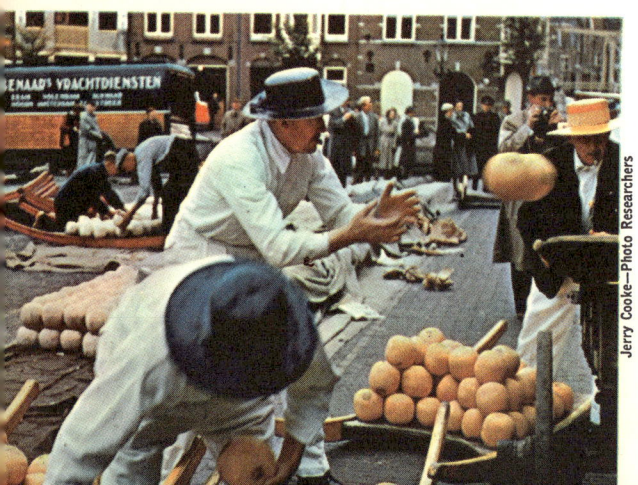

The famous weekly cheese market in Alkmaar in the Netherlands is popular with visitors.

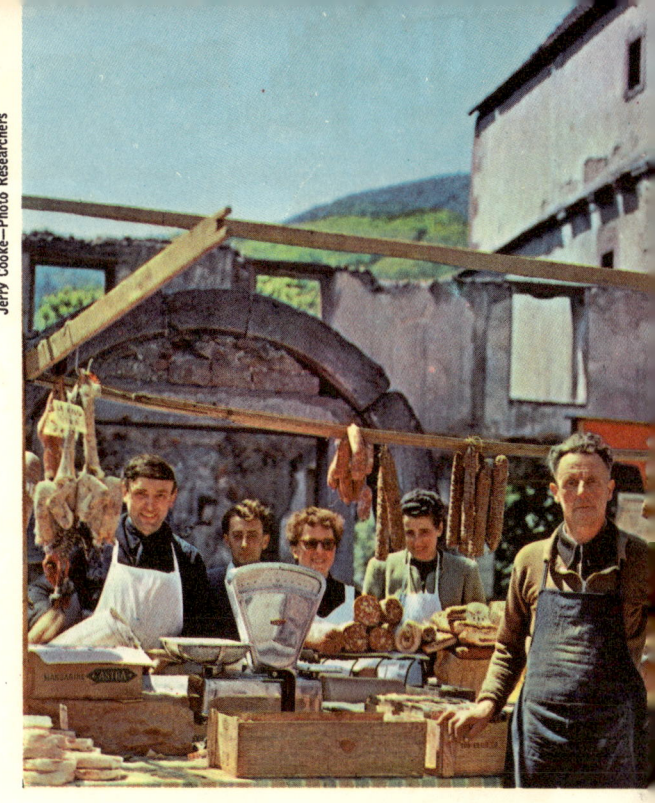

A sausage shop in Kaysersberg, Alsace. Each region of France has its food specialties.

Jerry Cooke—Photo Researchers

is drier than the west and north, and better for grains. The English also raise hops, vegetables, and fruits.

In France three out of ten people make their living from agriculture. Wheat is the most important grain crop. Northern France also raises many sugar beets and turnips. Where conditions are suitable, grapes are plentiful and many world-famous vineyards clothe the sloping hills.

Normandy and Brittany are well known for apples. Grasse, in the south, is noted for its flowers from which perfume is made.

Normandy is also famous for its dairy cattle. From their milk Camembert cheese is made. The French also produce many other popular cheeses.

The grape harvest is important in France. One out of every 25 acres is used for growing grapes.

David Forbert—Shostal

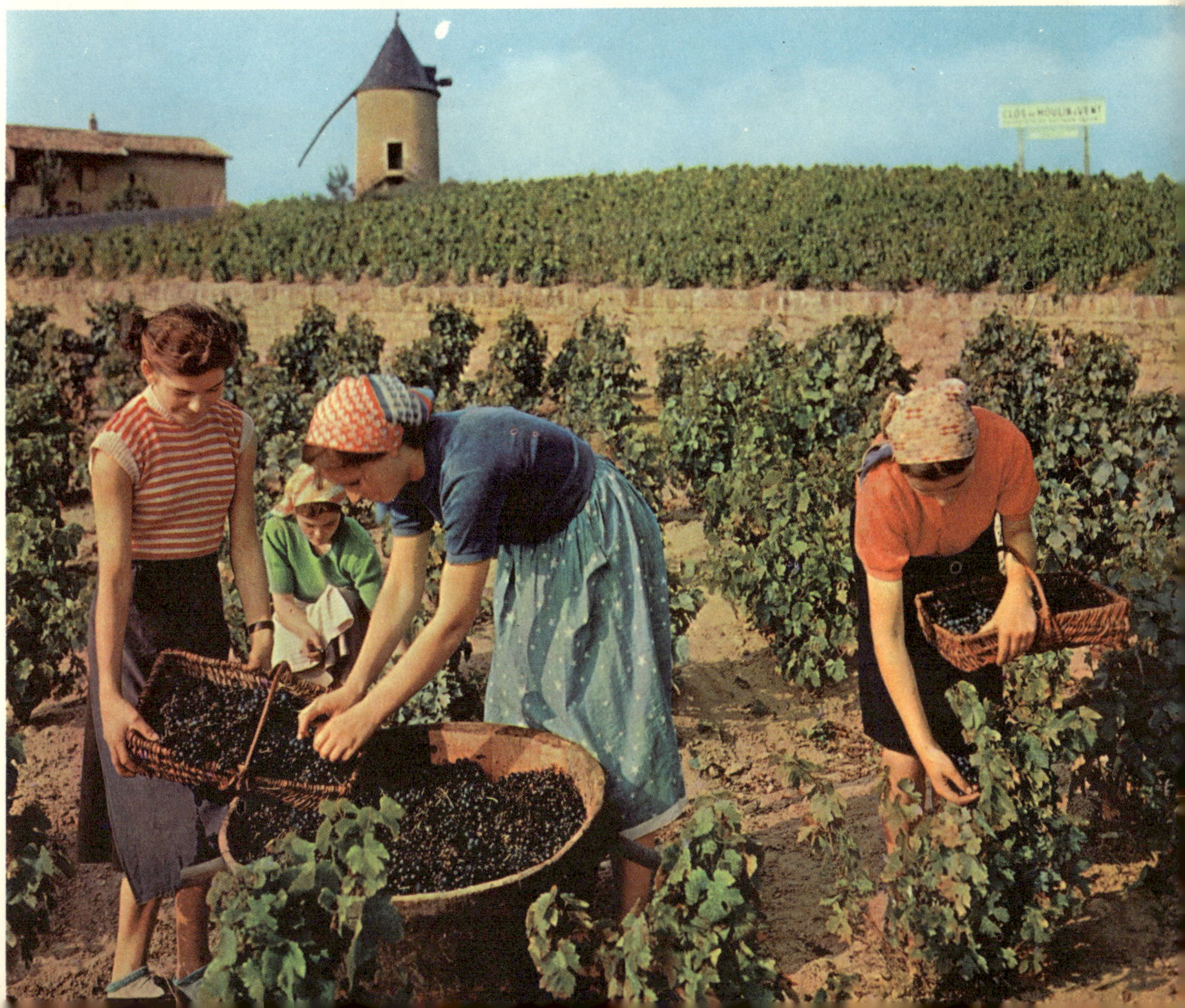

Ernst A. Heiniger

Cowbells tinkling from upland pastures are typical of Swiss hillsides and alpine meadows.

Northern France is noted for its heavy Percheron draft horses, which may weigh more than a ton.

Belgian farms are small. They average only five acres apiece. But they are the most productive in Europe. In addition to grains Belgium grows sugar beets, potatoes, tobacco, flax, and fruit. Cattle and horses are raised, particularly in the east.

Despite its important iron and steel mills, more than half the land of Luxembourg is used for agriculture. Farmers specialize in oats and potatoes, grapes, cattle, and pigs.

The Netherlands is world-famous for its tulips. They have been a Dutch specialty for 250 years. Other bulbs are grown, too. In spring the fields between Haarlem and Leiden are bright with many varieties of tulips, daffodils, and other flowers.

Swiss alpine hillsides also produce hay. Farmers feed it to their cattle during the winter.

Courtesy of TWA—Trans World Airlines

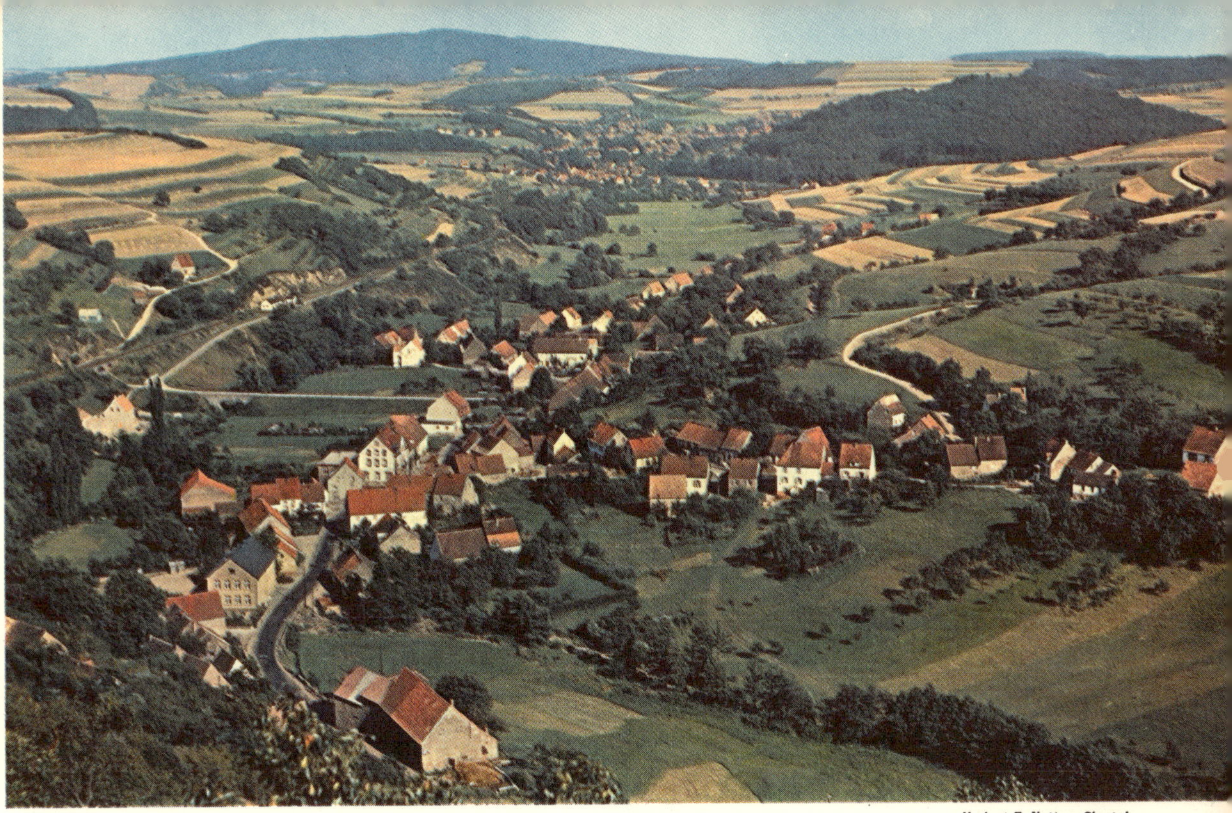

Herbert F. Nutter—Shostal

This farming village is in the Rhine Valley in West Germany, part of the fertile West European Plain.

Grains, potatoes, sugar beets, and vegetables are also raised.

Some 3,000,000 cattle graze the Netherlands' level fields. Grain to feed them in winter must be imported. Dutch cheeses are widely sold in Europe and America.

Germany, like most other areas in Western Europe, is a land of small farms. This is now true even in East Germany. The big estates of prewar days have been broken up and divided among the peasants.

In the central plain grain crops are popular. So are sugar beets and potatoes, and such specialties as flax. Some farmers grow hops which are used in making the beer for which Germany is famous. Fruits include apples, pears, and peaches. Many grapes are grown, too. Indeed, vineyards along the Rhine have been famous for a thousand years.

Stock is grazed on the slopes of the Alps and in many other places. Holstein, in the north, is famous for its cattle and has given its name to our best-known breed of black and white dairy cows.

Switzerland with its mountains and steep slopes is largely a grazing country. It is noted for its dairy products which include Swiss and Gruyere cheese. Austria is also a land of steep slopes, small farms, grazing, and dairy products.

Phillippe Doumic—Shostal

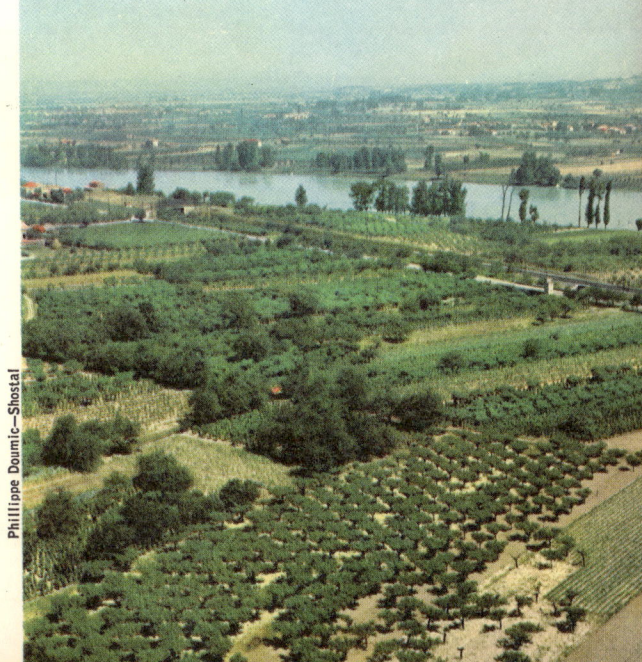

Fruits and vegetables are raised in the rich Rhone valley in southern France.

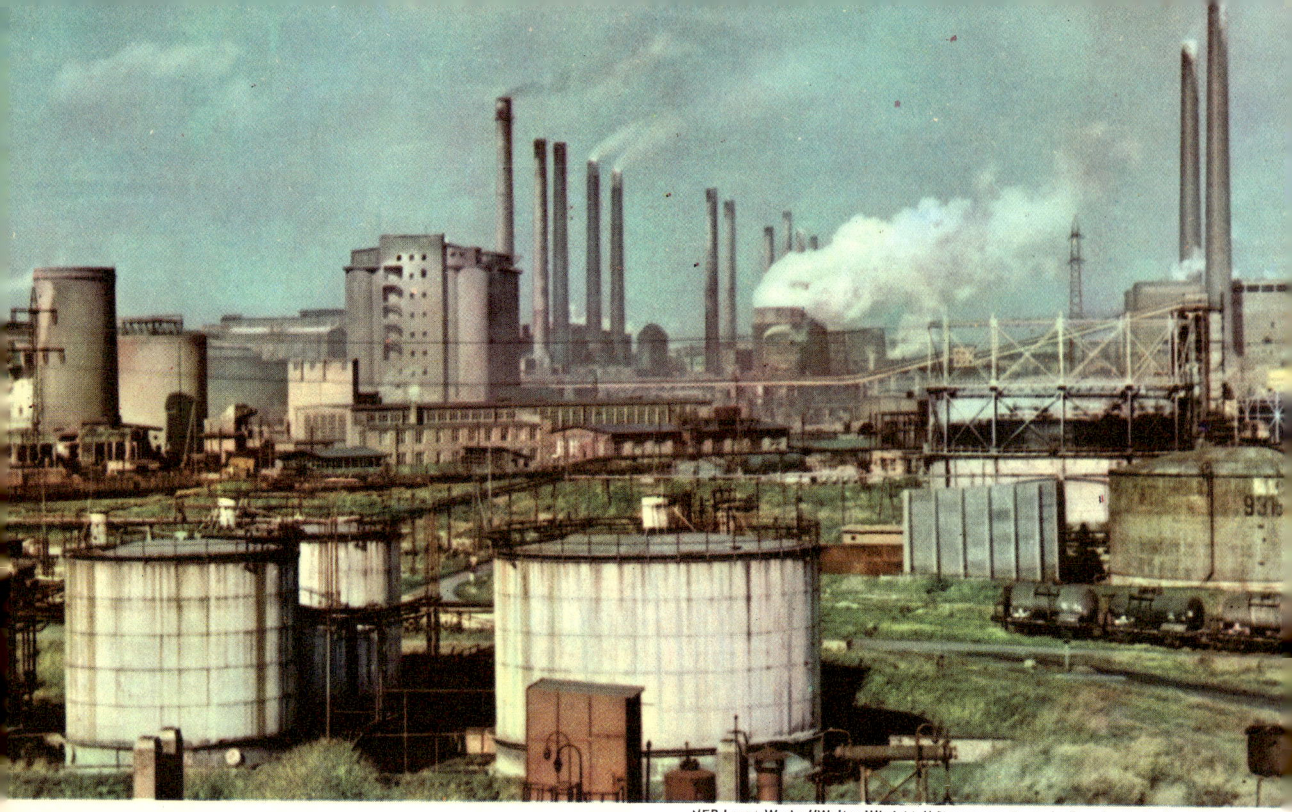

VEB Leuna-Werke "Walter Ulbricht," Merseburg, Deutsche Demokratische Republik

The Leuna works in Merseburg near Leipzig, East Germany, make chemicals out of coal.

Tom Hollyman—Photo Researchers

Mining and Manufacturing

Great Britain was the first country in the world to develop industries based on steam power. It was soon joined by France, Germany, and the Low Countries.

In the nineteenth century these nations soon reached leading positions in trade and manufacturing. This was due in part to the fact that in these countries coal and iron ore were found close together. It was therefore relatively easy to manufacture steel, machine tools, and machinery, on which all other manufacture depends.

The growing industries of Western Europe needed raw materials. Some were at hand, such as clay for making china. Others had to be imported from abroad. Of particular importance was cotton, which came from the southern United States, and wool, much of which came from Australia and New Zealand.

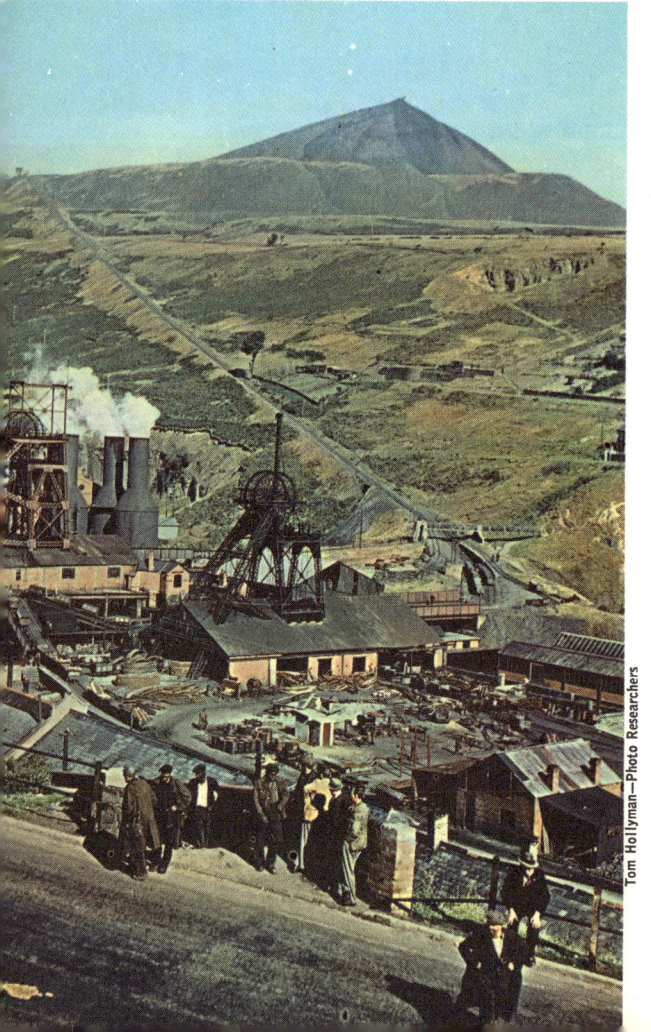

Many Welshmen work in coal mines like this one in the Rhondda Valley, the coal center of Wales.

This is the largest French steel mill. It is located at Rombas in industrialized Lorraine.

Demand for these—and for many other raw materials—increased activity in shipbuilding. With more ships came a growth of overseas trade and an increased interest in new markets abroad. Great Britain, France, the Netherlands, Spain, and Portugal, with much competition, had had some overseas colonies since shortly after the discovery of the New World. Trade with these colonies had long been important to the mother countries.

With the rise of manufacturing and industry the European countries added to their overseas possessions. In order to assure supplies of raw materials and to gain new markets, the mother countries divided up Africa. They also acquired new colonies in Asia. Many of these colonies, however, are now self-governing or independent. The same is true in Africa.

Shipbuilding in France. France is becoming more highly industrialized.

French railway mechanics at work. France has more than 25,000 miles of state-owned railroads.

Wolff and Tritschler—Shostal

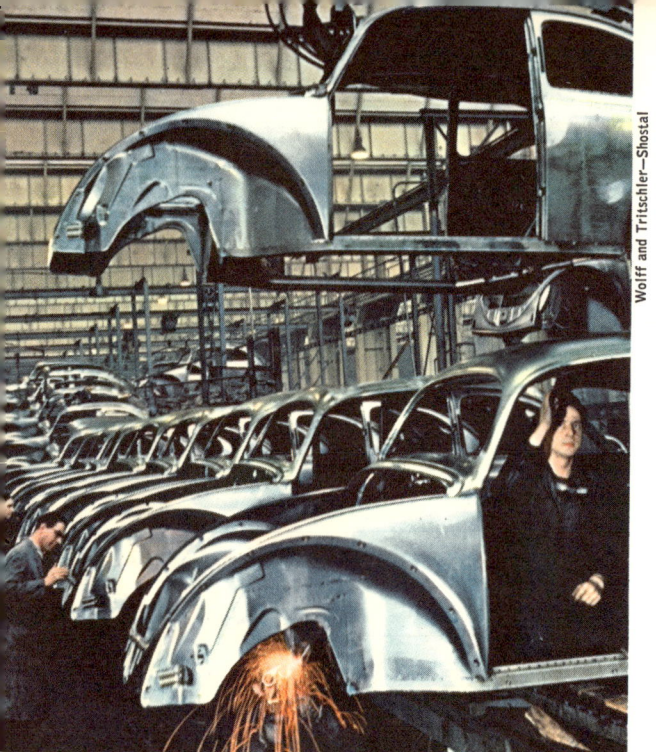

An assembly line in the Volkswagen factory

World War II destroyed many factories in Western Europe. These have now been almost entirely replaced by more modern plants. In spite of the growth of industries elsewhere, its heritage of skill and experience has helped keep Western Europe one of the great workshops of the world.

In Great Britain coal is mined in England and in Wales. In England the county of Yorkshire is noted for its woolens and the county of Lancashire for its cotton textiles. The city of Sheffield has long been famous for fine steel and the county of Staffordshire, with its good clay, for fine china. The great cities of Manchester and Birmingham are the centers of two of England's most important general manufacturing districts.

Britain accounts for one third of the world's shipbuilding and, next to the United States, has the world's largest merchant fleet. British exports include plastics, chemicals, metals, machine tools, electrical equipment, locomotives, automobiles, and airplanes. Britain is also a world leader in the use of atomic energy for peaceful means. It opened its first atomic power plant in 1955.

The docks of London occupy 35 miles of the banks of the Thames, England's longest river.

Aerofilms Limited

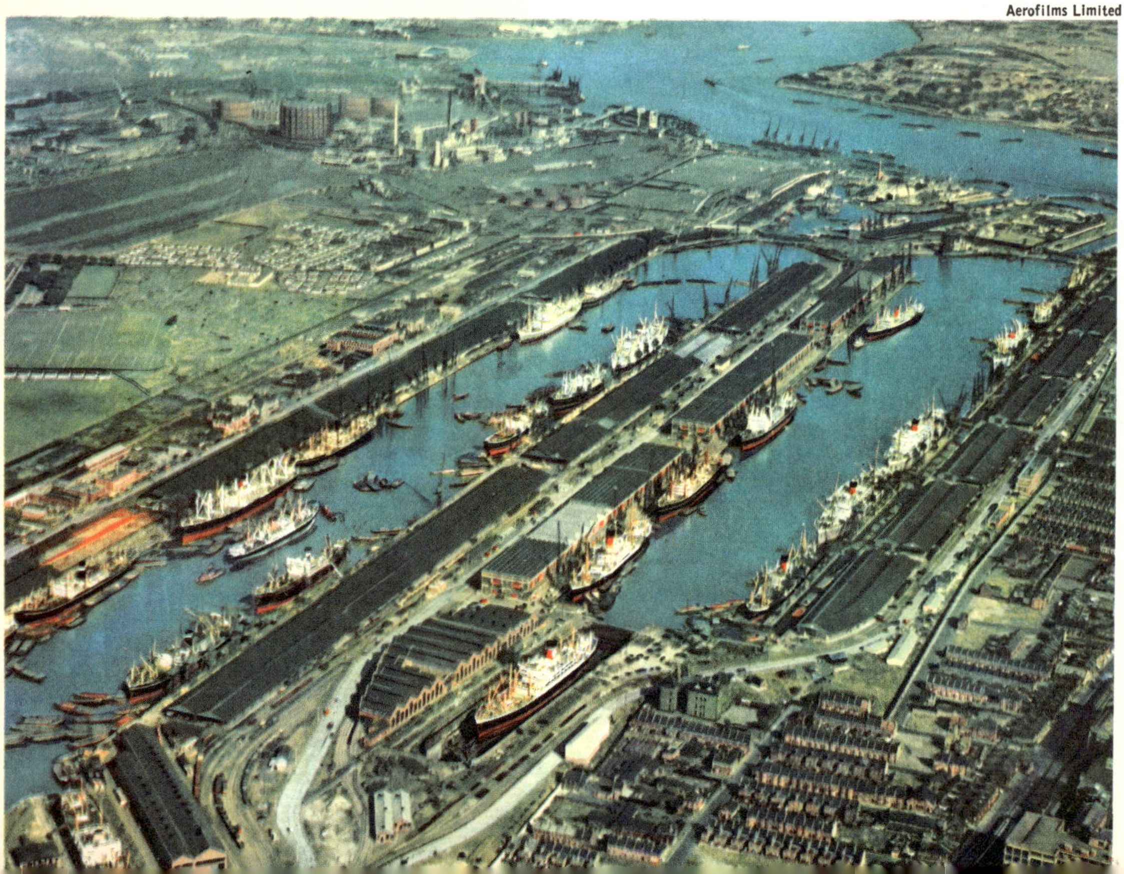

France has long been a center for fine arts and crafts. Fashionable women's clothes from Paris, cosmetics, perfumes, silk—these are some of the exports for which France is famous.

But France also has heavy industry. It has deposits of coal, iron ore, bauxite (for aluminum), clay, and potash. And there is cheap hydroelectric power from dams in the Alps.

In addition to fine handicrafts, French exports now also include a wide variety of manufactured goods, as well as some of the world's finest wines.

Belgium is an important manufacturing country with a large steel industry. Its exports include textiles, chemicals, and glassware. Brussels lace and Belgian chocolate are especially well known.

The Netherlands mines some coal and salt, and manufactures iron, steel, machines, and chemicals. The Netherlands also has great oil refineries. It is the world's third largest shipbuilder and a vast amount of trade with Germany goes through its ports. Amsterdam is the world's greatest diamond center.

Rich deposits of iron ore make Luxembourg, small as it is, one of Europe's important steel producers.

Germany's Ruhr valley is the biggest industrial area west of the Soviet Union. It has giant steel mills, automobile, locomotive, and machine tool factories, and many others. Both West and East Germany manufacture and export fine scientific instruments, toys, clocks, glassware, and pottery. Large potash deposits in West Germany are the base of a great chemical industry.

Switzerland makes and exports watches, toys, and milk chocolate. Austria is the largest producer of oil in Western Europe and leads the continent in the mining of magnesite. It also produces and exports iron and steel, as well as lumber, paper, textiles, glassware, leather goods, and electric power.

David Forbert—Shostal

German workers are noted for their skill. This craftsman makes cuckoo clocks.

Europe still has many handicraftsmen. This French cobbler specializes in wooden shoes.

David Forbert—Shostal

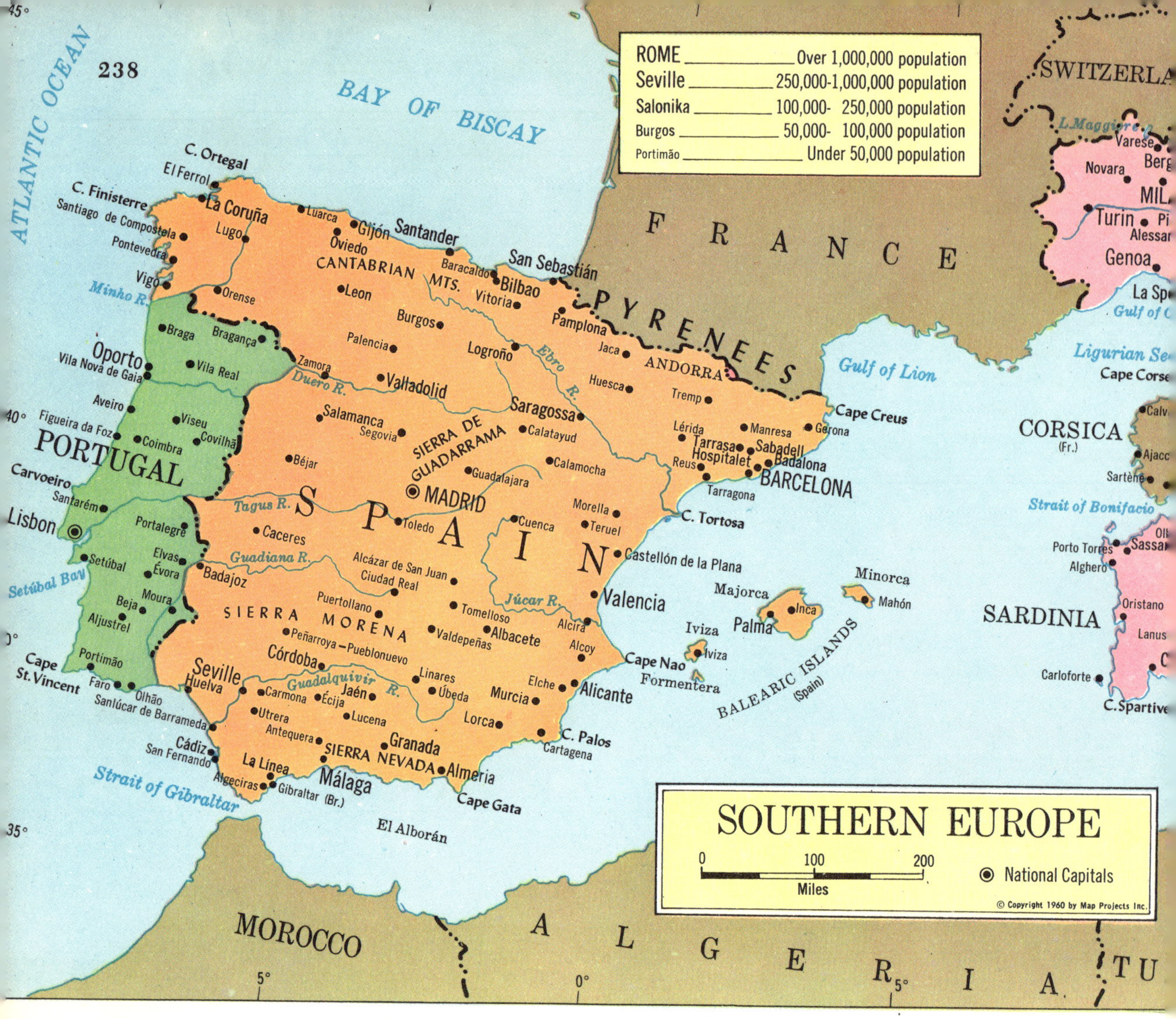

238

SOUTHERN EUROPE

ROME	Over 1,000,000 population
Seville	250,000-1,000,000 population
Salonika	100,000- 250,000 population
Burgos	50,000- 100,000 population
Portimão	Under 50,000 population

0 — 100 — 200 Miles

● National Capitals

© Copyright 1960 by Map Projects Inc.

Venice, Italy, is built on piles in a marsh. Canals serve as streets. "Taxis" are boats called gondolas.

Paulus Leeser—Camera Clix

SOUTHERN EUROPE

Southern Europe consists of Portugal, Spain, Italy, and Greece. Portugal and Spain occupy the Iberian peninsula. Italy and Greece also occupy peninsulas. The Madeira and Azores Islands in the Atlantic Ocean are part of Portugal. The Canary Islands in the Atlantic Ocean and the Balearic Islands in the Mediterranean Sea are part of Spain.

In addition to the republic of Italy, the Italian peninsula contains the tiny mountain republic of San Marino. Vatican City, the headquarters of the Roman Catholic Church, is an independent country of 109 acres within the city of Rome.

The Iberian peninsula is separated from the rest of Europe by the Pyrenees Mountains. Its southernmost tip is the rock fortress of Gibraltar that guards the entrance to the Mediterranean. Gibraltar is owned by Britain. Britain also owns the island of Malta near Sicily.

Italy is separated from the rest of Europe by the Alps, which form its northern frontier. The Italian peninsula juts out into the Mediterranean like a leg with a high-heeled boot about to kick the island of Sicily as a football. Sicily and the island of Sardinia are part of Italy.

The peninsula of Greece is divided in two by the isthmus of Corinth. The southern part is called the Peloponnesus. The island of Crete belongs to Greece. So do the many islands in the Aegean and Ionian Seas. Greece, including her islands, has the longest coastline of any country in Europe.

This Spanish city still preserves the walls which protected it in medieval days.

Southern Europe has less rain than Western Europe. Most of it falls in the mild winter. The summers are dry and hot. Such a climate is good for winter resorts, but not for crops, unless they can be irrigated.

At one time Southern Europe was well wooded. For hundreds of years, however, men cut more trees than they planted. Because the climate is rather dry, trees do not grow back rapidly. Overgrazing often prevented the growth of young trees. Today much of the countryside is bare of trees.

With no woods to hold back the rain as it falls the water rushes off the land taking soil with it. Erosion, as we call this washing away of the soil, has destroyed much formerly fertile farm land. This makes the land poor and the farmer poor. It is one reason for the poverty in Southern Europe.

The long coastline of Southern Europe early turned the attention of its people to the sea. The Greeks, Romans, Portuguese, and Spaniards in turn were great overseas merchants. But today their countries have fallen behind Western and Northern Europe in maritime trade. All, that is, except Greece. In recent years Greece has come to the fore as an important seafaring nation.

Much of Southern Europe is upland or mountainous, and is better suited for grazing than for agriculture. The best lands for farming are along the river valleys or the coasts. But, for reasons we shall see, agriculture in general is backward in Southern Europe.

The heavily fortified Rock of Gibraltar rises 1,400 feet above the entrance to the Mediterranean.

SOUTHERN EUROPE 241

Nazaré, a Portuguese fishing town, overlooks the Atlantic. Fishing is an important industry in Portugal.

There are many rivers in Southern Europe. A few, such as the Ebro and Guadalquivir in Spain and the Po in Italy, are fairly long. But most are relatively short. They flow down steeply from mountains nearby and are navigable only for short distances. Famous rivers in Southern Europe include the Tiber, which flows by the city of Rome, and the Tagus, which flows by the city of Lisbon.

Small villages at the foot of rugged mountains are typical of the Greek countryside.

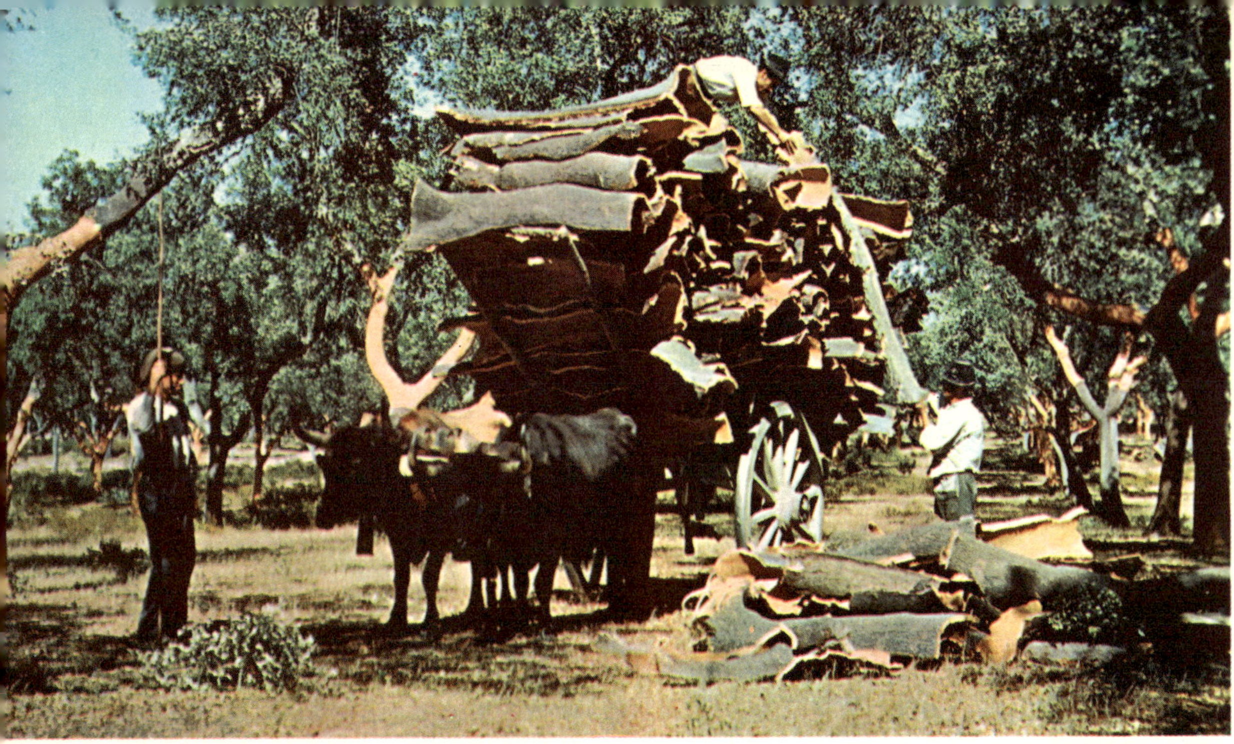

Ed Drews—Photo Researchers

The outer bark of Portuguese cork oaks is taken away on oxcarts. Cork is made from this bark.

Use of the Land and Sea

In Southern Europe more than half the people make their living from the land. But it is usually a poor living.

The backwardness of agriculture in Spain, Portugal, and southern Italy is partly due to the system of land ownership. Huge estates are often owned by absentee landlords, who may live in Lisbon, or Madrid, or Rome. They do not spend much time on their properties, and they take little interest in introducing modern methods of agriculture.

In other parts of Southern Europe, farm land is often either mountainous or it is in a densely populated river valley. In both cases farms are apt to be too small to benefit from the use of modern machinery. (The average Greek farm, for example, is only 5 acres.) This is another reason why farmers in this area are likely to be poor.

The climate and soil of Southern Europe are especially good for grapes. Spain and Italy together have more than 6,000,000 acres of vineyards. Most grapes are made into wine.

Portuguese farmers raise the grapes that are made into port wine. From Madeira comes the well-known Madeira wine. Sherry is made from the grapes of southern Spain. In the heavily cultivated Po Valley of Italy, grape vines are trained over the farmers' houses and strung along the paths. In Greece some grapes are dried and sold as raisins and currants.

Wendy Hilty—Monkmeyer

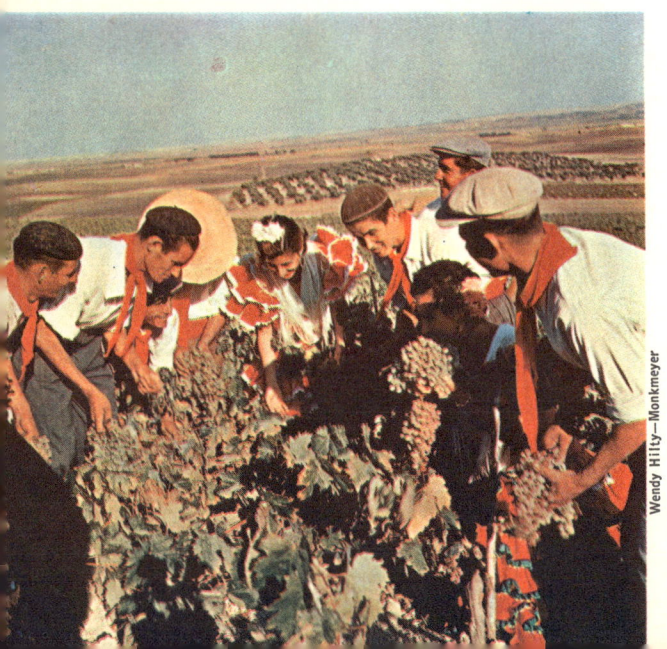

These newly harvested grapes in southern Spain will be made into wine, Spain's chief export.

Such old-time sights as this waterwheel well are still seen in the Spanish countryside.

Courtesy of TWA—Trans World Airlines

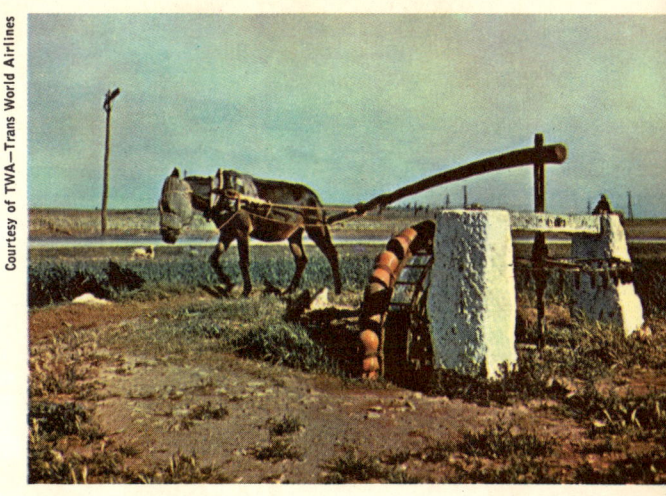

The climate and soil of Southern Europe are also good for olive trees. Their gray-green groves cover dry hillsides all around the Mediterranean. Olive oil often takes the place of butter in these countries. Italy leads the world in the production of olives.

Citrus orchards are popular in Southern Europe. In Spain they are most common along the Mediterranean coast. Sicily is noted for its lemons.

The roast chestnuts sold on city streets in North America come from Spain or Italy. In these countries, many hillsides are planted with chestnut trees, and chestnuts are an important food item.

Almonds, figs, and dates come from the warmer parts of Southern Europe. To the north, in the Po Valley, many Italian farmers grow mulberry trees to feed silkworms.

As in ancient days, however, wheat is the most important crop. After wheat come corn, barley, oats, rye, and rice. Barley will grow where it is too dry for wheat. Oats and rye are often raised in mountain areas. Rice is grown in lowlands where rivers provide water for irrigation.

Olive groves cover hillsides along the banks of the Genil River in Andalusia, southern Spain.

Josef Muench

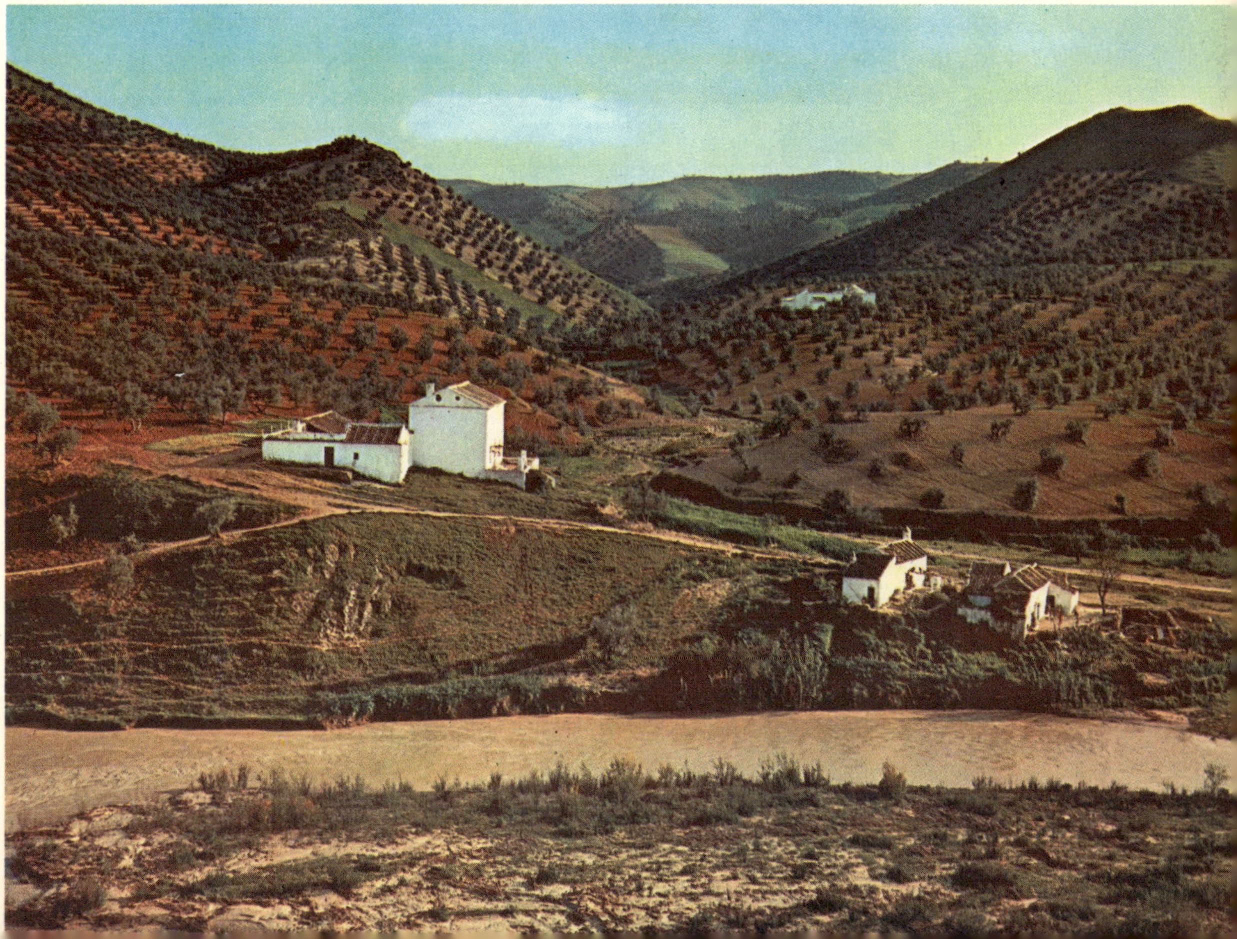

Rice fields in the Po Valley, an important rice-growing region in Lombardy, northern Italy

Spain and Italy each have some 10,000,000 acres in wheat. Because of Spain's dry climate and old-fashioned farming methods, the yield is less than one third of what French farmers raise on an equal area. Portuguese grow wheat on their central highlands. Most Italian wheat comes from part of the Po Valley known as the "breadbasket of Italy."

Beans, potatoes, sugar beets, and other vegetables are also planted in suitable areas, including valleys of Spain that were first irrigated by the Moors. On the Mediterranean coasts of Spain and Italy many fruits and vegetables are raised. The fertile Po Valley is the richest agricultural region in Italy. The Macedonian Plain, with its cotton and tobacco, is the best farming land in Greece.

In the southwestern and northeastern parts of the Iberian peninsula grows the cork oak. This peninsula accounts for most of the world's supply of cork, which comes from the bark of this tree.

Centuries of overgrazing have helped reduce the timber resources of Southern Europe. The overgrazing is in part due to goats and sheep. They are far more common in Southern Europe than elsewhere in Europe.

Sheep, and especially goats, can live on much worse land than can cattle. Therefore, as land has become poor through unwise use, goats have been able to thrive and give milk where cattle could not. But they have often thrived at the expense of the land. They will eat every green blade in sight and not give new trees or vegetation a chance to get started.

The mountains and many uplands of Southern Europe are better adapted to grazing than farming. Cattle are raised in northern Spain and on the slopes of the Alps in Italy. From the milk of Italian cows several fine cheeses are made, and cheese is important in the Italian diet.

Bulls for bullfighting are raised in southern Spain. Herdsmen in central and western Spain breed Merino sheep, noted for their excellent wool.

In Southern Europe oxen and donkeys are still widely used on farms, where in Northern and Western Europe we would be likely to see tractors or horses.

An orange grove in Sicily perches on the slopes of Mt. Etna, an active volcano.

SOUTHERN EUROPE 245

Joe Barnell—Shostal

Ox-teams pull harvesters in a northern Italian wheatfield. Oxen are still used on many Italian farms.

Fish form a large part of the diet and exports of Portugal. Her fishing fleet numbers more than 16,000 vessels. Many of them, of course, are rather small. Some catch herring in the nearby Atlantic. Great numbers of young herring, called sardines, are canned in olive oil and exported. Other Portuguese fishermen bring in tuna and cod. Many of the cod are caught on the Grand Banks off Newfoundland.

Fishing is less important in Spain. On the northwest coast, however, there is a sardine fishery, and Spanish fishermen also catch some tuna.

The Mediterranean Sea flows into the Atlantic Ocean at the Strait of Gibraltar through a narrow and shallow opening 11 miles wide and only 1300 feet deep. This means that the deeper waters of the Mediterranean do not receive from the Atlantic

Greece is a land of many sheep and goats. Flocks along the road are a common sight.

Herbert Lanks—Monkmeyer

Divers gather sponges from the shallow sea bottoms around Greece and her islands.

Ewing Krainin—Photo Researchers

Courtesy of the Johnson Motor Company
A Portuguese fishing boat with its sardine catch spread on racks to dry in the sun

Amleto Fattori, Filmeco, Rome, Italy
Sardinian fishermen harpooning trapped tuna fish. Many tuna are caught in the Mediterranean.

the cold currents which are so important for the production of fish food.

Fishing in the Mediterranean, therefore, is rather poor. And the long coastlines of Italy and Greece do not support a great fishing industry, as do the long coastlines of Northern Europe. However, small quantities of fish are still caught for local consumption. Tuna is the leading catch.

The people of the Mediterranean coasts have been sailors and traders since the earliest times we know of. Today, shipping is an important source of income for the Southern European countries. Greece and Italy, especially, have large fleets of freight and passenger ships. The Greek-owned merchant fleet (not all under the Greek flag) ranks third in the world.

Along the Mediterranean, salt is evaporated from sea water and processed, as here at Trapani, Sicily.
Ernst Kleinberg—Shostal

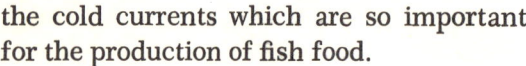

Ancient Crafts and Modern Industries

Southern Europe is a land where many things are still made by hand, as they were long ago. The visitor to Portugal can see big markets full of handmade pottery and handmade furniture. He can watch workers fashioning beautiful tiles, and women making beautiful lace. If he goes to Madeira he will see the embroidery for which the island is famous.

The visitor to Spain and to other parts of Southern Europe will see many of the same sights. The making of embroidery and pottery by hand, for example, are widespread occupations all through the region.

Italy is famous for its craftsmen. Those in Florence specialize in jewelry and leather work. Venice is known for its fine glass and lace. In Rome skilled workers make many religious art objects. The cutting of cameos is popular around Naples.

All over Italy one sees beautiful carvings in ivory and alabaster, and sculptures in marble. Other Italian crafts include fine pottery and mosaics. Italians have a reputation for good workmanship.

In countries like these, that are just beginning to be industrialized, the first factories are usually those dealing with food processing. Thus in all Southern Europe, for example, the making of olive oil and wine are major industries. The next factories to be built are usually textile mills. We find some of these now in Southern Europe.

In Portugal the canning of sardines is important. Spain and Italy have refineries for making sugar from sugar beets. The Italians are famous for the wide variety of foods they make from flour. Their manufactured food products include spaghetti, ravioli, macaroni, and noodles.

Northern Italy is the most industrialized region in Southern Europe. This is especially true of the cities of Milan, Turin, and Genoa. In part this is due to water power from the Alps, in part because this region is

Duncan Edwards—FPG

Lacemaking is a common art in Southern Europe. Here is an open-air worker at Taormina, Sicily.

A glass blower at Murano, near Venice. Since 1292 Murano has been famous for its glassware.

Terry S. Lindquist—FPG

Joe Barnell—Shostal

Automobiles are manufactured in northern Italy. This is the Fiat test track at Turin.

Italy's volcanic Mt. Etna supplies high-grade lava for use as building stone.

Duncan Edwards—FPG

nearest the rich markets of Western Europe. In part it is also due to the recent discovery of natural gas in the Po Valley.

Automobiles, motorcycles, and motor scooters are important products. So are machine tools, sewing machines, typewriters, business machines, and chemicals. Northern Italy is the leading steel-producing center of the peninsula.

Italy has little wealth in minerals. It does, however, mine coal in Sardinia and a little iron ore from the island of Elba. Heavy industry depends on coal from abroad and hydroelectric power from the Alps. Italy is noted for its output of Carrara marble, which is used by sculptors. Sicily has sulfur and a little oil.

Greece has only simple industries—a few food-processing and cigarette factories.

Southern Europe is a land of contrasts. In one place village women sit in the shade making lace by hand. In another, great mills turn the night sky red as they roll out steel for locomotives.

Italy manufactures large numbers of motor scooters for customers at home and abroad.

David Forbert—Shostal

EASTERN EUROPE

Dubrovnik, Yugoslavia, is a port and bathing resort on the Dalmatian coast of the Adriatic Sea.

EASTERN EUROPE

Eastern Europe includes all the countries east of Germany and Austria and west of the Soviet Union. These are Poland, Czechoslovakia, Hungary, Romania, Yugoslavia, Bulgaria, and Albania. They stretch from the Baltic Sea to the Black Sea.

The Poles, Czechs, Slovaks, Yugoslavs, and Bulgarians are Slavic peoples and speak Slavic languages. The Romanians speak Romanian, a language derived from Latin. The Hungarians and Albanians speak separate languages of their own.

Because it is farther from the moderating influence of the ocean, Eastern Europe has hotter summers and cooler winters than Western Europe. The land is relatively flat in most of Poland, Hungary, northern Yugoslavia, and southern Romania. The rest of the region is largely mountainous.

The principal rivers are the Oder and Vistula, which flow north into the Baltic

Budapest is two cities: Buda, an old fortress town, and Pest, an industrial city across the Danube.

250 EASTERN EUROPE

Traditional peasant costumes can still be seen in Bulgaria's remote mountain villages.

Communist May Day paraders march through the streets of Prague, capital of Czechoslovakia.

Sea, and the Danube, which flows east into the Black Sea. Eastern Europe has less coastline and less fishing and maritime trade than any other part of Europe.

Most of the people in these countries make their living from the land, as their fathers did. Industry is important only in Czechoslovakia and Poland.

Eastern Europe lies in the pathway of the migrations of people from Asia into Europe. For hundreds of years it has been swept by invasions and wars. These unsettled conditions have held back progress. Until recently land was owned by powerful landlords in large estates. Farming methods were backward. The farmers—and indeed most of the people—were poor.

At the end of World War II the Russian Army drove the Germans out and occupied these countries. The Russians set up Communist governments. These new governments introduced a socialist way of life in which the government (rather than private individuals or companies) owns industries and the land. These new governments also encouraged industry and collective farming, as we shall see below.

Great changes are taking place in Eastern Europe. But at a distance from the towns and fertile plains many of the old ways may still be seen.

Fields of potatoes stretch mile after mile across the flat plains of Poland.

Jerry Cooke—Photo Researchers

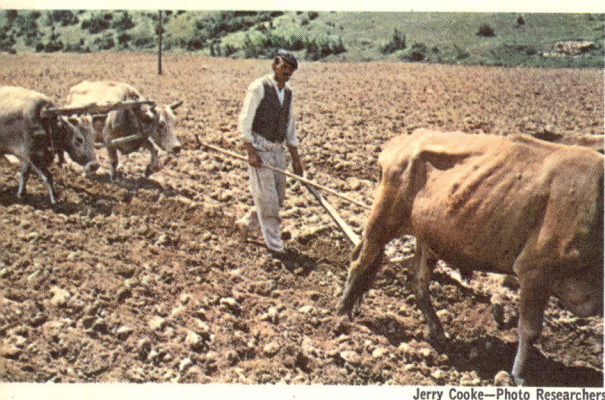

This Yugoslavian farmer plows with oxen, but Yugoslavs are using more tractors each year.

Changing Farmlands

Before World War II, Eastern Europe had for a long time been a region of small farms and great estates. In the mountains and foothills and in narrow river valleys the farms were small. On the plains of Poland and along the broad Danube valley there were great estates.

After the war the big estates were broken up. Then, in many places, groups of individual farms were grouped together into collective farms. In much of the region this process is still going on.

Eastern Europe is largely agricultural. Only two countries—Poland and Czechoslovakia—have any great amount of industry. Elsewhere from half the people (as in Hungary) to nine out of ten of the people (as in Albania) make their living from the land.

Wheat is the most important crop on level or rolling lands. But barley, oats, rye, corn, potatoes, and sugar beets are also raised. Poland is second only to the Soviet Union in the world production of rye and potatoes.

Much of the southern part of Eastern Europe is rugged. Livestock grazes on hillside pastures. Some of this stock is cattle. But there are many sheep and goats.

From the milk of their goats (and sometimes cows) Bulgarians make a famous sour milk dish called "yogurt." Hungarians take pride in their championship cattle. Poland and Czechoslovakia also raise cattle and each has an active dairy industry. Poland and Yugoslavia produce many hogs.

Although these Bulgarians harvest wheat by hand, machines are replacing hand labor in Eastern Europe.

Marilyn Silverstone—Palmer Photo Agency

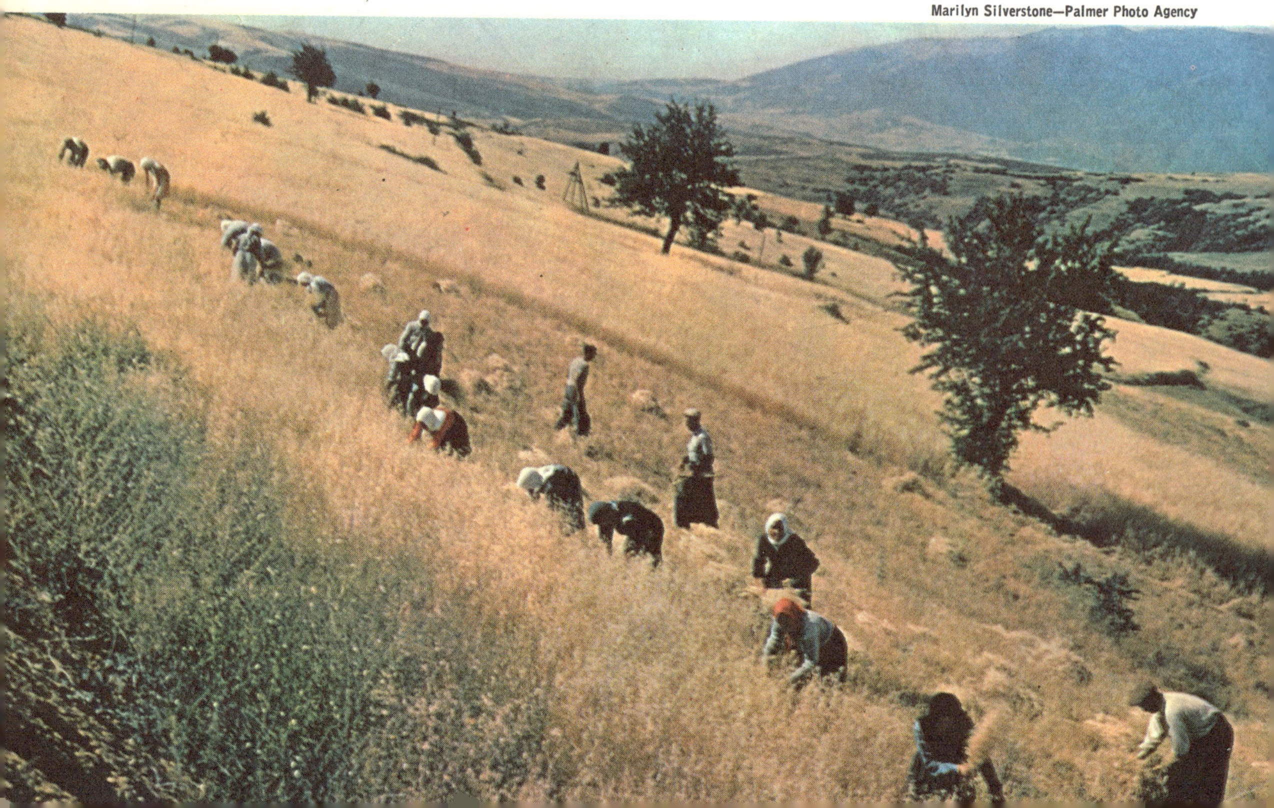

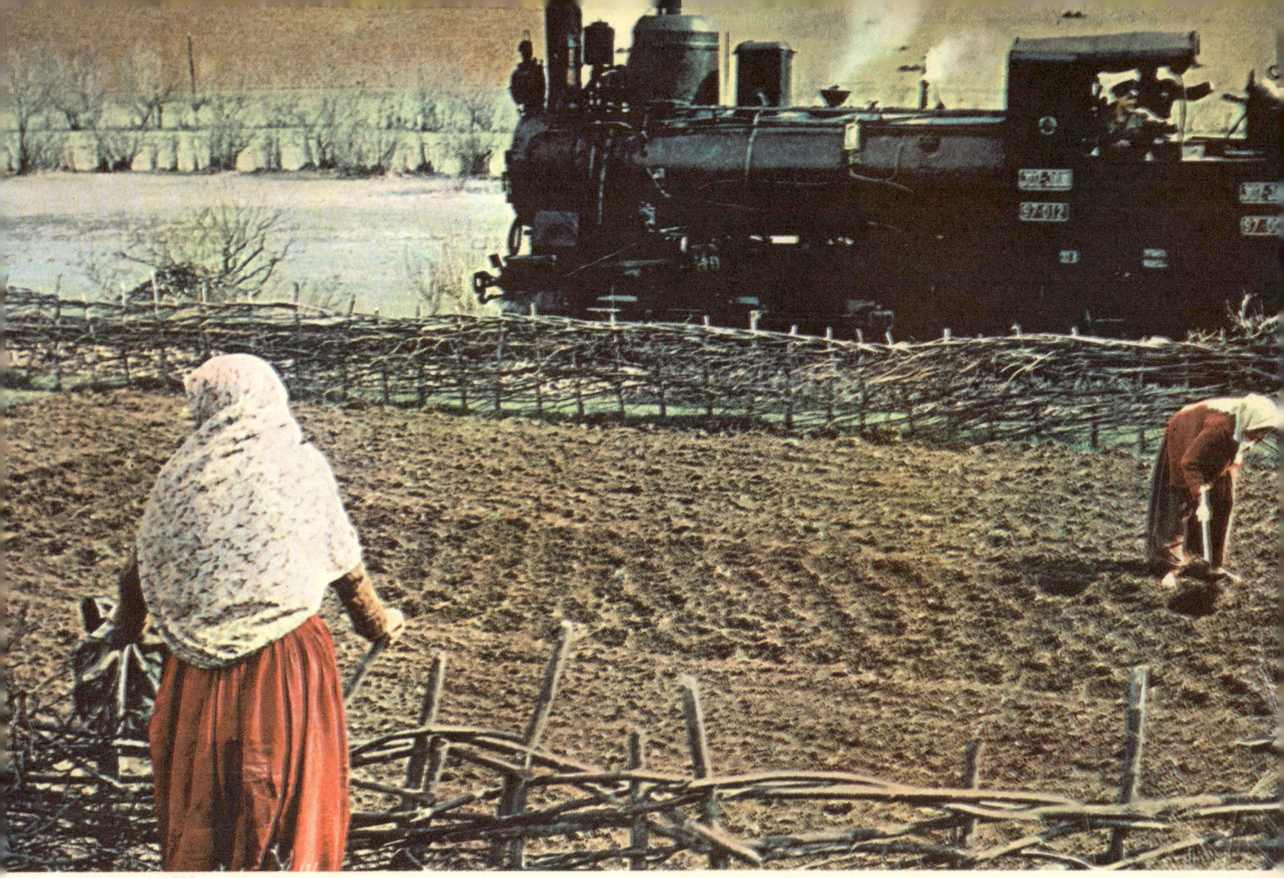

Edwin Nysfrom—FPG

Old-fashioned shawls and hand labor contrast with a steam locomotive in Yugoslavia.

Every country has some crop in which it specializes. Bulgaria is famed for its roses from which rose oil, called "attar of roses," is made. It is used in perfumes.

Czechoslovakia grows many hops. They go into the brewing of Pilsener beer for which the country is famous. Hungary is known for its Tokay wine and paprika, a kind of red pepper. Poland is famous for its hams. Many of them are sold abroad.

From the delta of the Danube in Romania comes the sturgeon, a fish whose eggs are made into caviar. Yugoslavia and Bulgaria are noted for a special plum brandy called "slivovitz."

Almost every Eastern European country has large forests. Most also have a scientific forest conservation program. The purpose of the program is to make sure that

John Strohm

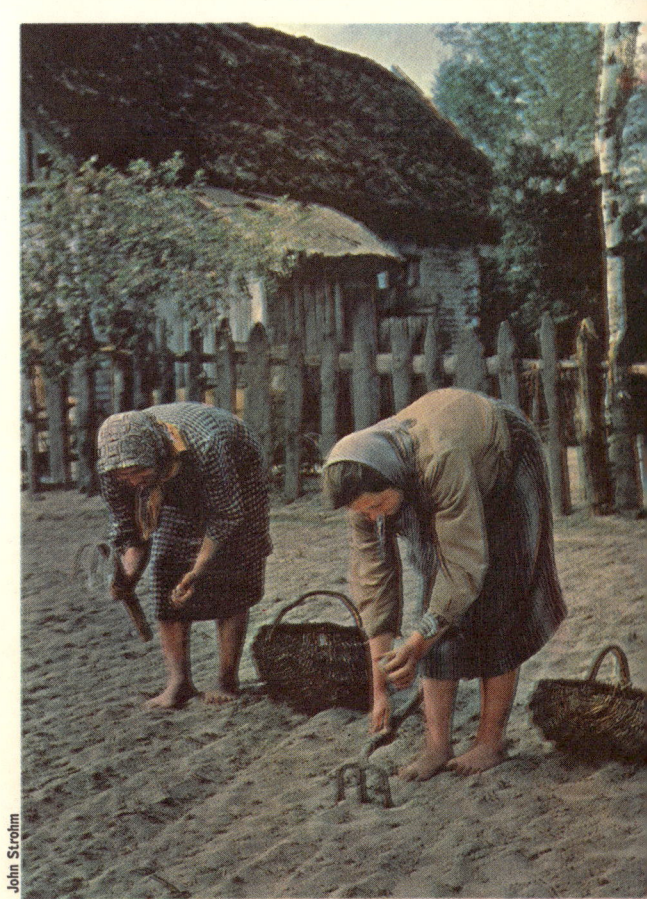

Planting potatoes in Poland. There are still many small farms in Poland, despite collectivization.

254   EASTERN EUROPE

there will be plenty of timber that can be cut each year without destroying the forest.

Since the end of World War II most of the farmland in Bulgaria, Romania, Hungary, and Czechoslovakia has been collectivized. We will learn more about collective farms in the section on the Soviet Union.

In Poland and Yugoslavia collective farms were started on a large scale but did not prove popular. Many farmers were allowed to go back to working their individual farms themselves. It is too early to tell to what extent collective farms will be adopted in these two countries.

In all the countries of Eastern Europe machines are gradually taking the place of hand labor and draft animals on the farms. This is true whether the farms are collectivized or not, although the collective farms are the ones that get the new machinery first.

Important changes are still taking place in the agriculture of Eastern Europe—more than have taken place in any part of the European countryside for many years.

Eastfoto

Haying with mechanical farm equipment on a collective farm in Czechoslovakia

This collective farm in Czechoslovakia uses both horses and machines—a sign of changing times.

John Strohm

Industry in Eastern Europe

Eastern Europe has much less industry than Western Europe. Most of it is in Czechoslovakia and Poland. Each of the other countries has a little, except Albania, which has almost none.

Two things are important about industry in Eastern Europe: (1) it is growing rapidly, and (2) it is largely government-owned.

Before World War II, Eastern Europe was principally an agricultural region. The Communist governments that took power after the war were anxious to industrialize these countries. They felt that having strong industries was the only way they could remain in power and the standard of living of the people be improved.

In order to build a strong industry a country has to spend money for machines, not for new clothes. So people often have to go without many consumer goods—the things that in the United States one can buy at a five and ten cent store or a department store. Since the war every country in Eastern Europe has built a number of new industries and enlarged old ones. Many countries have made a point of heavy industry—iron, steel, machinery, and machine tools. These are the products that help build more factories. When heavy industry is built up, the governments allow more consumer goods to be made.

This rapid increase in industry in rather poor countries took place because the governments, being dictatorships, could enforce it. The governments gradually took over, or nationalized, the larger private businesses in each country. Sometimes they paid the former owners for them. More often they did not.

Governments also put money into new industries. In most countries a planning board was set up to see to it that all the different government-owned businesses worked efficiently together. Sometimes the planning worked well. But not always.

Eastfoto

A steel mill in the industrial city of Ostrava, Czechoslovakia, near the Silesian coal mines

This new Polish steel mill at Nowa Huta is expected to make 2,000,000 tons of steel a year.

Paul Hufner—Shostal

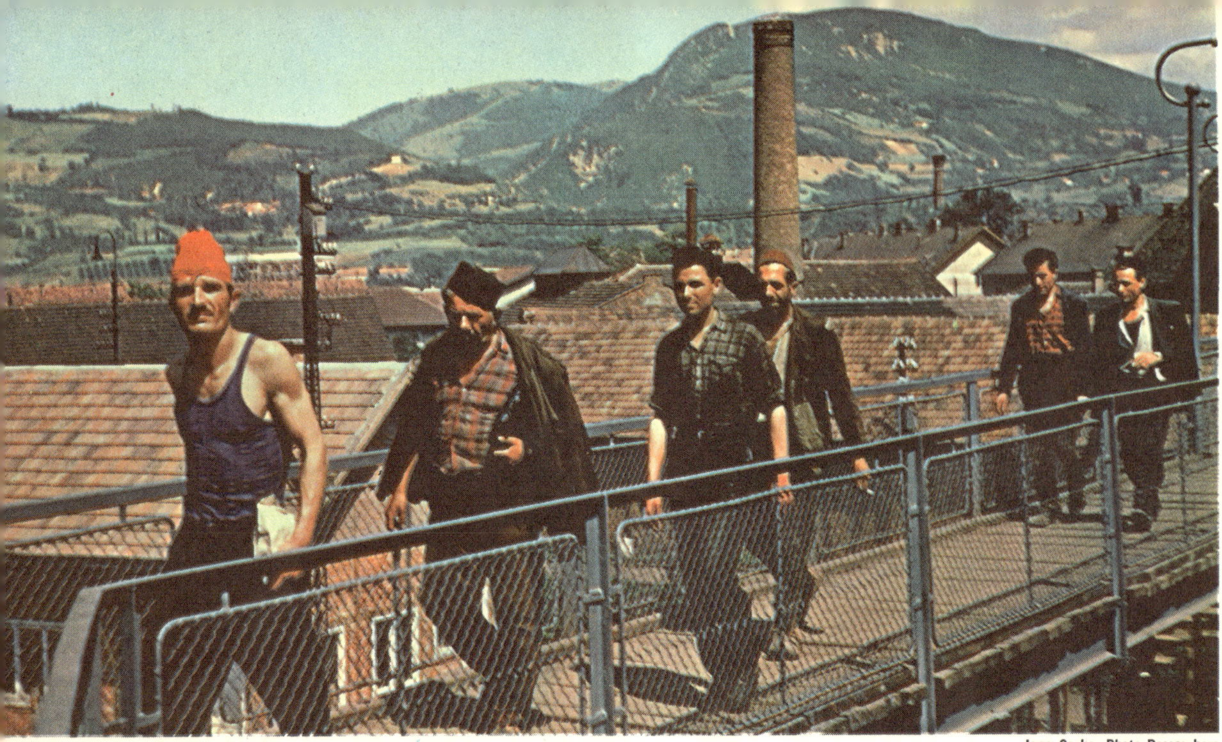

Jerry Cooke—Photo Researchers

Steel workers in Yugoslavia—signs of the industrialization of Eastern Europe since World War II

At first the governments only took over the largest companies and the most basic industries, such as iron and steel. Later they took over smaller businesses.

In most Eastern European countries private owners are still allowed to operate the smallest businesses. The laws vary in different countries. In some, a private owner can—or could—employ up to 50 workers. In other countries he can only employ up to 10. In general, though, the governments are taking over more and more private businesses. Sometimes the former owner is kept on as manager.

These changes in ownership and the building of new plants do not always involve great changes in the kinds of goods produced. Except for an increase of heavy industry, each country still has its own specialties.

In Bulgaria most factories are engaged in the processing of agricultural products.

Manufacturing locomotives and railway cars, as at this factory, is one of Hungary's industries.

Eastfoto

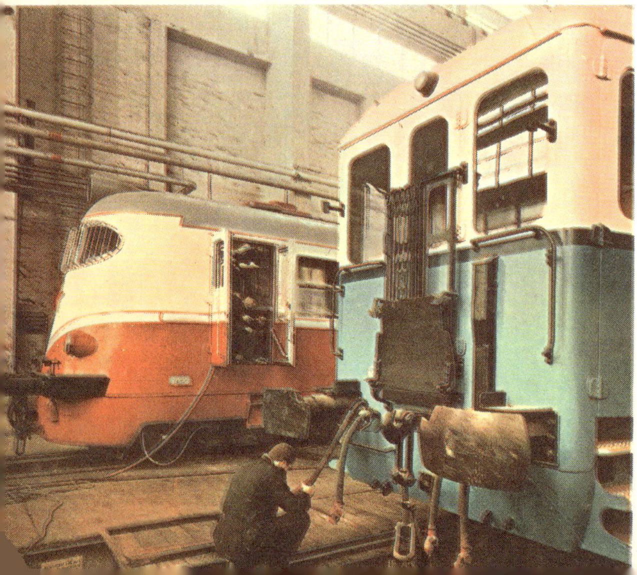

A rose distillation plant in Bulgaria. 435 pounds of petals make one ounce of rose oil.

Paul Hufner—Shostal

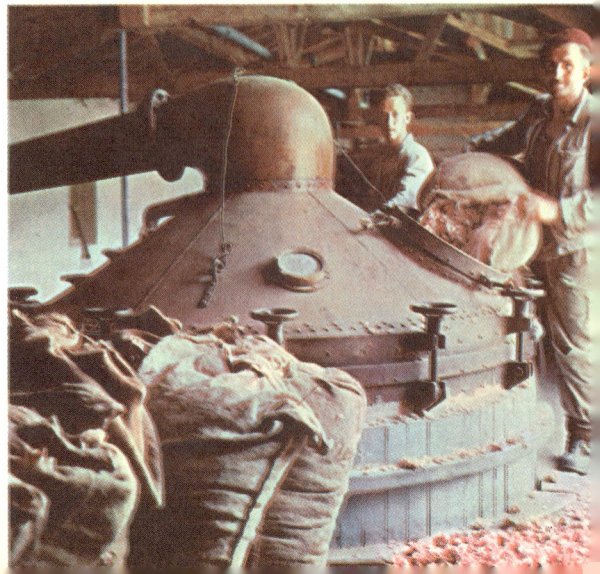

EASTERN EUROPE 257

Weaving is an important home industry in eastern Europe. These are Bulgarian rug-weavers.

Much of this is refined at the great oil center of Ploesti. Romania also mines some coal, iron, and salt. It has rather small but growing industries in metals, textiles, and food processing.

Yugoslavia has a limited amount of heavy industry in Slovenia and Bosnia, in the western part of the country. Light industries include lumber, furniture, and beet-sugar refining.

Yugoslavia also has valuable mineral deposits. It leads Europe in the production of antimony, lead, and bauxite.

As a result of the new factories there has been a considerable increase in production in Eastern Europe since the war. Conditions of life often remain difficult. But the region is becoming more and more industrialized and some additional consumer goods are being manufactured.

But some new metals and machinery factories have been built. Coal mining is the principal mineral industry.

In Czechoslovakia one out of three persons works in industry. Two great factories are widely known—the Skoda munitions works and the original Bata shoe factory. Czechoslovakia has a strong iron and steel industry. It also exports machinery, textiles, glass, china, and chemicals.

In Hungary, like Bulgaria, most manufacturing is the processing of agricultural products. But heavy industry, though still small, is being encouraged. Poland has great steel mills. It manufactures machinery, locomotives, farm equipment, chemicals, and textiles. It has Europe's largest coal mines, as well as lead and zinc.

Romania is the biggest European producer of oil outside of the Soviet Union.

Hungary imports raw cotton, but its own mills manufacture all its textiles.

Courtesy of the Fiat Company
The giant Fiat plant in Turin symbolizes the spread of industry to Europe's undeveloped areas.

Britain is a leader in the peaceful use of atomic energy. This plant is at Calder Hall.
British Information Service

EUROPE'S FUTURE

In Europe there are more different countries in fewer square miles of land than there are in any other part of the world. Almost every one of her 30 countries has a different language. Many of them have quite different cultures. All of them charge special taxes, called tariffs, on goods coming in from almost all other nations.

Over the centuries, Europe's nations have fought many wars against each other. Today many hatreds still linger on. What does the future hold?

First of all, the future depends upon peace. If the nations can learn to settle their disputes peacefully, the future is bright. But war—and particularly nuclear war—would kill millions of people and destroy much of Europe's as well as the rest of the world's civilization.

Since the modern nations came into being, great changes in man's control over nature have taken place. We now have railroads and superhighways, airways and jet lines, telegraph, telephone, radio, and television. All these have brought the countries of Europe much closer together than they were 150 years—or even 25 years—ago. The Europe of the future will have to reflect these changes.

The tariffs between nations that once were so important now often seem like troublesome barriers to trade. Already today some of the countries are forming economic unions and common market areas. Such common markets encourage mass production, and, as a result, more and cheaper goods. Some people even look forward to one free market for all Europe.

Will this mean that each country would give up its independence? Hardly. But today most nations seem willing to submit to an international authority in areas where they think it will be to their interest. Some statesmen have even urged the different countries to join together in a United States of Europe.

Would a closer union mean the end of the different cultures of Europe? No. Indeed, in a peaceful and prosperous Europe, each country should be able to develop its own culture more fully.

In Southern and Eastern Europe the future will probably see more efficient farming methods and greater industrialization. Around the Mediterranean there should be more reforestation. With the growth of jet air travel Northern Europe will become more important for flights across the Arctic from North America and Asia.

Will the geographical position of Europe —so valuable in the age of ship travel—be less important in an age of travel by air? The answer is probably no. Europe today has a great network of airlines and will probably have still more.

The peaceful use of atomic power in the future should be of special benefit to coun-

Tom Hollyman—Photo Researchers

The Hansa section of West Berlin. Modern architecture is typical of new German construction.

tries such as Italy and Greece that have little coal or oil. Finally, greater use of the sea—one of the important, scarcely-tapped resources of mankind—should help those countries of Europe with long coastlines.

Europe has had a brilliant history. If it can keep the peace, its future should be even brighter.

New superhighways like Germany's famous Autobahn may provide closer links for Europe's nations.

Tom Hollyman—Photo Researchers

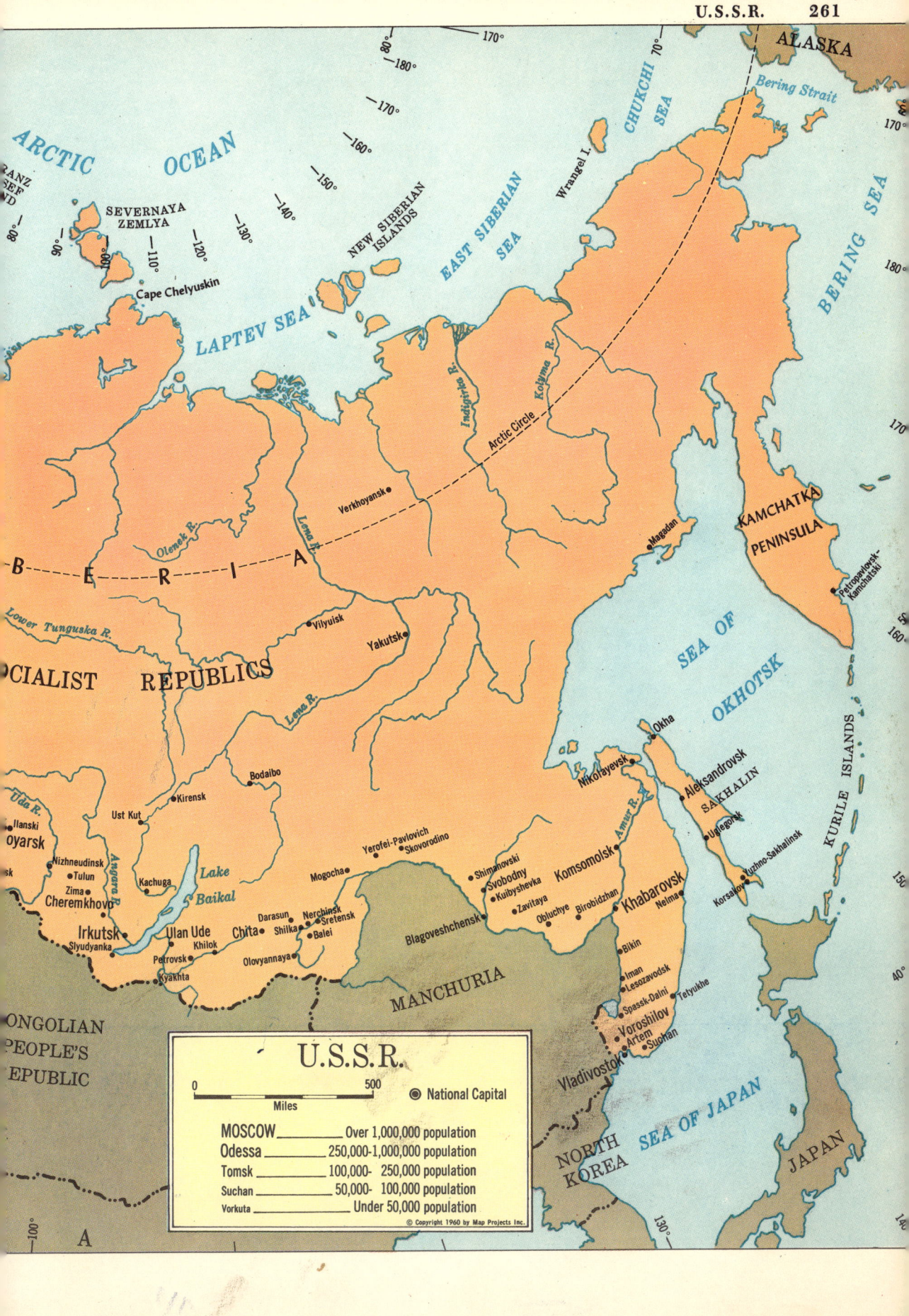

THIS IS THE U.S.S.R.

The Union of Soviet Socialist Republics, or U.S.S.R., is the largest country in the world. It occupies one seventh of the earth's surface.

It is located in both Europe and Asia. It stretches from the borders of Finland, Poland, and Romania to the Pacific Ocean. Its southern borders are the Black Sea, Iran, Afghanistan, China, and Outer Mongolia. The Arctic Ocean washes its northern frontier.

The Soviet Union, as it is also called, is a federation of 15 different republics. The Russian Soviet Federated Socialist Republic is by far the largest. The U.S.S.R. is a rich country. In its vast area of 8,597,000 square miles it contains almost all the resources needed for a modern civilization.

The 1959 census gave the Soviet Union a population of 208,000,000. Most of its people live in an area shaped like a triangle that stretches eastward from her western frontier to a point near Lake Baikal in Asia.

Most of the Soviet Union's coastline is on the Arctic Ocean and is ice-bound 10 months of the year. Many of the other

The 6,000-mile-long "taiga" in the U.S.S.R. is the largest evergreen forest in the world.

A wheat field on the 1,200-mile-long West Siberian Plain, one of the largest level areas on earth

Marilyn Silverstone—Palmer Photo Agency

Soviet sheep graze on the 12,000-foot-high plateau of the Pamirs, "the roof of the world."

ports require ice-breakers in winter. The fact of not having convenient all-year ports has affected Russian policy throughout its history.

In the U.S.S.R., plains stretch from the Polish border to central Siberia, as the Asiatic part of the Russian Republic is called. Uplands and mountains extend from central Siberia to the Pacific. The Caucasus, Pamirs, and other mountain ranges mark the southern frontier. The Urals stretch north and south, and mark the conventional boundary between Europe and Asia. Actually the Ural Mountains are quite low. They do not form a real barrier between the European and Asiatic portions of the U.S.S.R.

The largest Soviet river in Europe is the Volga, which flows south into the landlocked Caspian Sea. The Dniester and the Dnieper flow through the Ukraine into the Black Sea. The Ob, Yenisei, and Lena are huge Siberian rivers. But they all flow north into the Arctic Ocean. Therefore, they have not proved very useful for travel or for trade.

An ice sheet once covered the northern half of the Soviet Union in Europe. It left behind it many lakes and marshes. But most of Siberia was too dry for glaciers to

Lake Ritsa, high in the pine-clad Caucasus of Georgia, is a favorite Soviet resort.

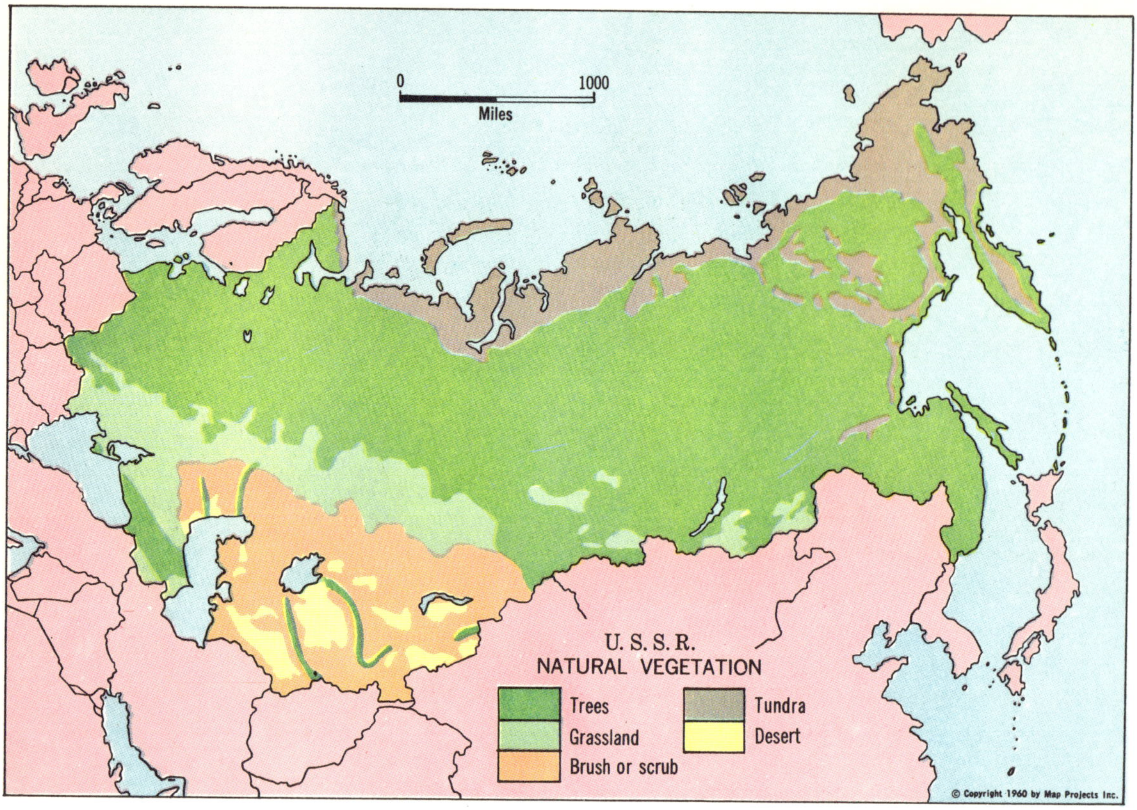

U.S.S.R.

U.S.S.R. NATURAL VEGETATION
- Trees
- Grassland
- Brush or scrub
- Tundra
- Desert

© Copyright 1960 by Map Projects Inc.

form. Instead, the cold permanently froze the soil. Such land is called "permafrost." Only the surface melts in summer. Permafrost covers 3,728,000 square miles of the U.S.S.R. This means that nearly half of the land area is underlain with permanently frozen soil. It is very difficult to grow crops over this frozen subsoil.

This village street scene is typical of hundreds of villages on the fertile plains of the Ukraine.

D. Lex

Marilyn Silverstone—Palmer Photo Agency

Pleasant countryside near Alma-Ata, capital of the Kazakh Republic, Soviet Central Asia

Harrison Salisbury—Photo Library

A barge on the mighty Volga, longest river in Soviet Europe, now dammed to make electric power

The history of Russia started about one thousand years ago. Powerful nobles were gradually brought under the control of a king, or czar, whose capital became Moscow. Conditions of life for most of the people were hard. The government treated them harshly. Discontent was widespread.

The first World War went badly for Russia. In 1917 a revolution broke out and the czar was overthrown. The Bolshevik Party under Lenin finally seized power. The Russian Empire, in the years that followed, came to be known as the U.S.S.R. The Bolsheviks were Communists. Their economic theories taught them that factories and land should be owned by the government, not by private individuals or companies.

Lenin and his followers were strong, able men. They would let nothing stand in the way of carrying out their theories, even if it caused great suffering. Stalin succeeded Lenin. He was cruel and suspicious, but he made the country strong in industry and he collectivized the farms.

Today the U.S.S.R. is, next to the United States, the most powerful nation in the world.

Fishing boats on the Caspian Sea. A favorite catch is sturgeon, whose eggs are eaten as caviar.

U. S. S. R. Magazine—Sovfoto

266 U.S.S.R.

CLIMATE

The climate of the Soviet Union is the most severe of any country of Europe. In Soviet Asia it is more severe still. That means long cold winters, short hot summers, and little rain or snow.

The Soviet Union is a northern country. Cape Chelyuskin is farther north than the tip of northern Alaska. Most of the Soviet Union is in the same latitudes as Canada. Its southernmost village, on the Afghan border, is only as far south as San Francisco. As a result, in most of the country the growing season is short and winters are long.

Another reason for the severe climate of the U.S.S.R. is the huge size of its land mass. Land takes up heat faster, and loses it faster, than the sea. Therefore, the bigger the land mass and the farther it is from the sea, the more it heats up in summer and the colder it gets in winter. One of the coldest towns in the Soviet Union, and perhaps in the world, is Verkhoyansk, in the middle of Siberia. It has had a record low winter temperature of 90 degrees below zero.

The Crimean and Caucasian coasts of the Black Sea are exceptions to the severe climate. They are sheltered by mountains and have a "mediterranean" climate with mild rainy winters and hot dry summers.

Because it is so far from unfrozen seas, the Soviet Union has rather little rain, except in the mountains. Most of this comes from the Atlantic Ocean from clouds that have already blown across Europe.

The western part of the Soviet Union receives about 20 inches of rain a year. This is enough for crops. But when the average falls lower, crops are uncertain or require special methods of dry farming. The low rainfall of 8 inches a year means that, without irrigation, much of Soviet Asia is a desert.

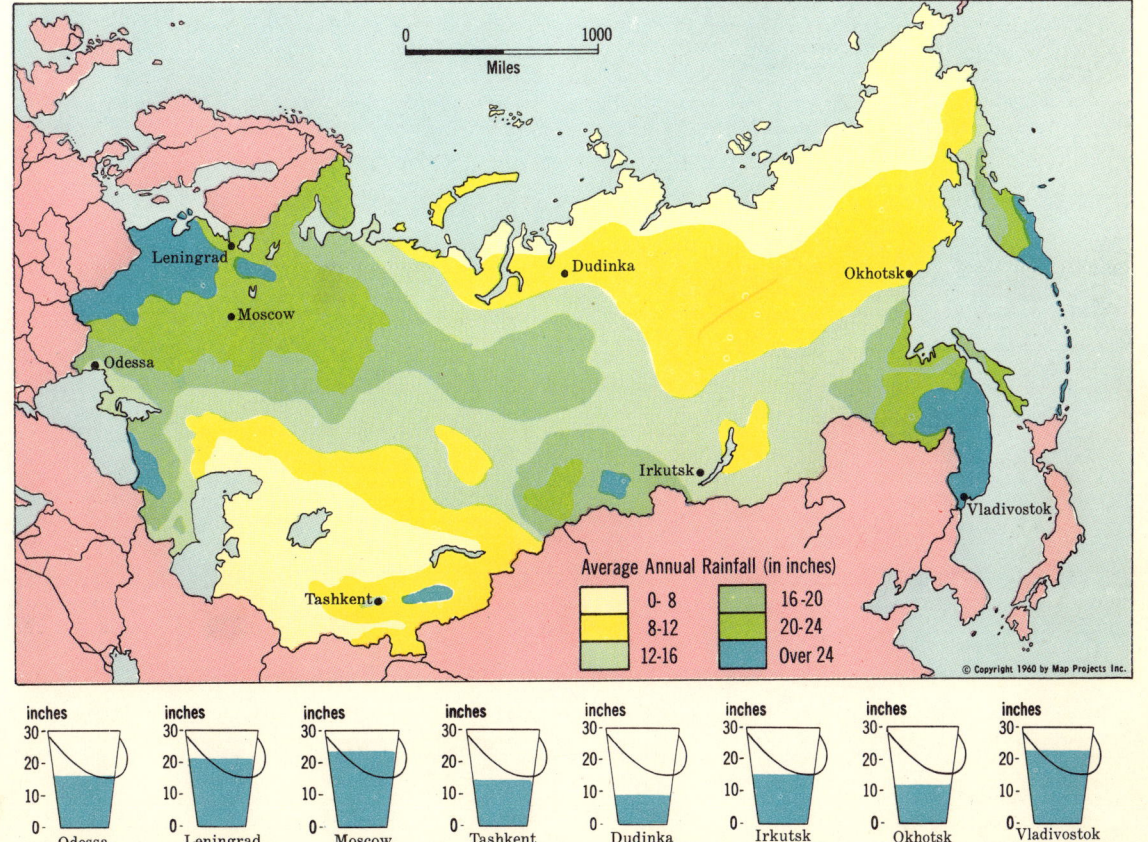

J. D. Winbray—Shostal

People from all over the U.S.S.R. come to Red Square, Moscow, to visit Lenin's tomb.

PEOPLE OF THE SOVIET UNION

The Soviet Union has more different peoples than all the rest of Europe. Each of its 15 "Union Republics" is of a different nationality. Each may include within its borders smaller self-governing regions. Each of these will have a different culture and language.

This is in keeping with the principle that people with the same language and culture should have their own local government. Therefore a study of the different republics and self-governing areas of the Soviet Union gives us some idea of the different peoples that it includes.

Russians are the principal nationality. In general, they have a sturdy body, rounded head, light hair, and bluish or gray eyes. They account for half the population of the Union.

Most live in the Russian Republic, which occupies three quarters of the area of the Union. But some Russians are found in other parts of the Union outside the Russian Republic.

The Russian Republic also includes a number of other nationalities. The Bashkirs, Chuvashes, Tartars, and Yakuts, for example, are of Turko-Tartar ancestry. Each has a theoretically self-governing republic of its own. Actually, all important orders come from Moscow.

Next to the Russians the Ukrainians are the largest nationality group. They number about one fifth of the total population of the Union. They live in the Ukrainian Soviet Socialist Republic, or the Ukraine. This lies in the southwestern part of the

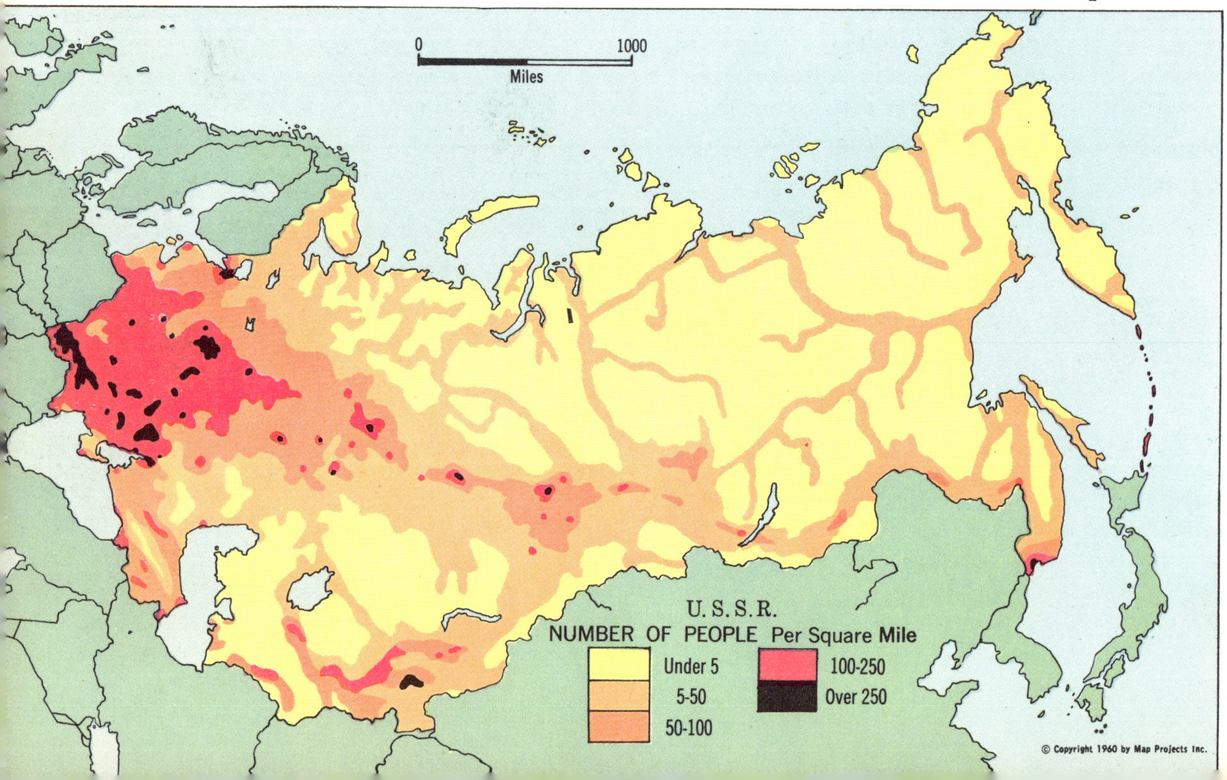

U.S.S.R.
NUMBER OF PEOPLE Per Square Mile
- Under 5
- 5-50
- 50-100
- 100-250
- Over 250

© Copyright 1960 by Map Projects Inc.

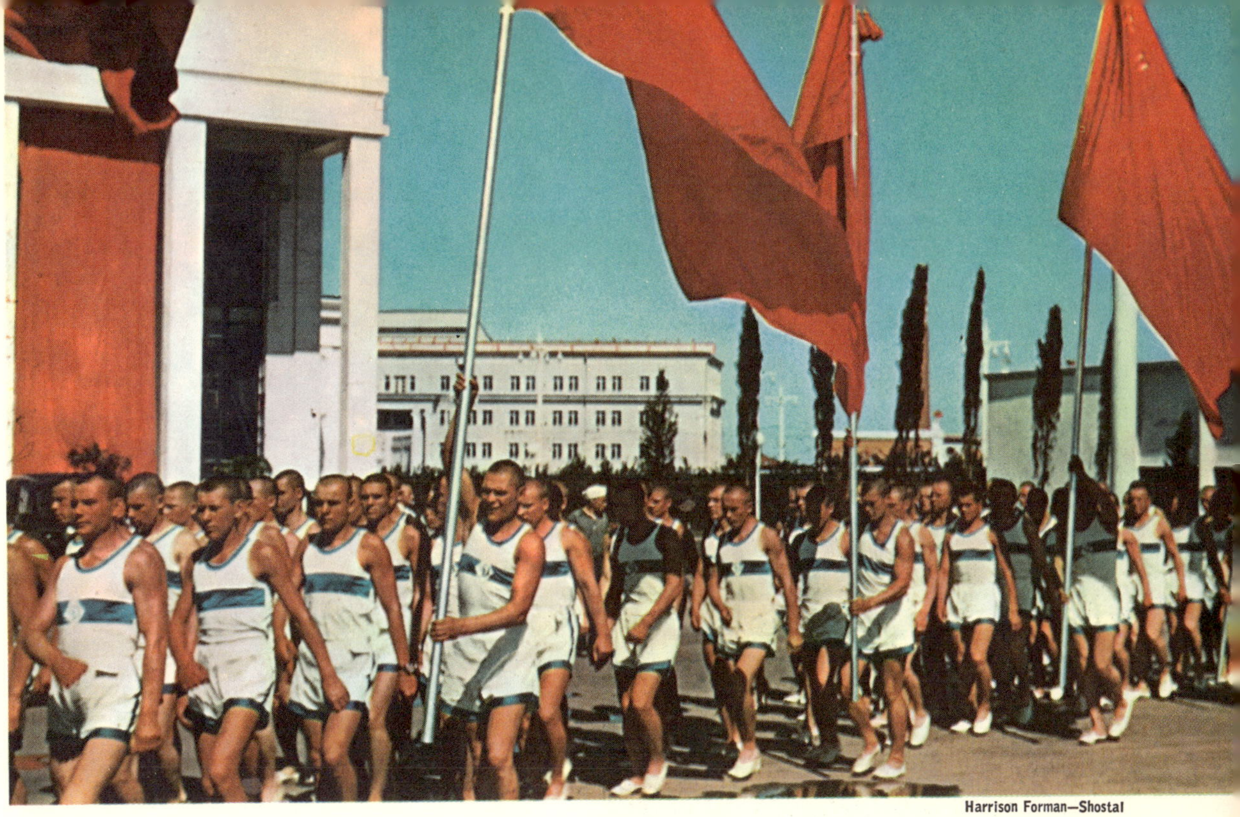

Harrison Forman—Shostal

The Soviet Union lays great stress on bodily fitness. Here is a physical education parade.

Union. It is sometimes called "the breadbasket of the Soviet Union" because of its vast, fertile fields.

North of the Ukraine the Byelorussians live in a land of lakes and marshes. Their 5,000,000 people form the third largest nationality group.

The Russians, Ukrainians, and Byelorussians are Slavs. Their languages are different, but related. Their principal religion is the Greek Orthodox Church. They are an eastern division of the Slavic cultural and language group to which, as we saw earlier, the Poles, Czechs, Slovaks, Yugoslavs, and Bulgarians also belong.

The Turko-Tartars are an important cultural and language group in the Soviet Union. They have rather high cheekbones, dark hair, and dark skin. This group includes most of the peoples of Central Asia such as the Turkmens, Uzbeks, Kazakhs, and Kirghiz. They are mostly Moslems.

Each of these nationalities has its own "Union Republic," some of which cover vast areas. The Kazakh Republic, for example, has 1,061,000 square miles. It is about the size of the United States east of

A boy tends his water buffalo in Georgia, a Soviet republic between Turkey and the Caucasus.

Robert Lackenback—Jim Quigney Associates

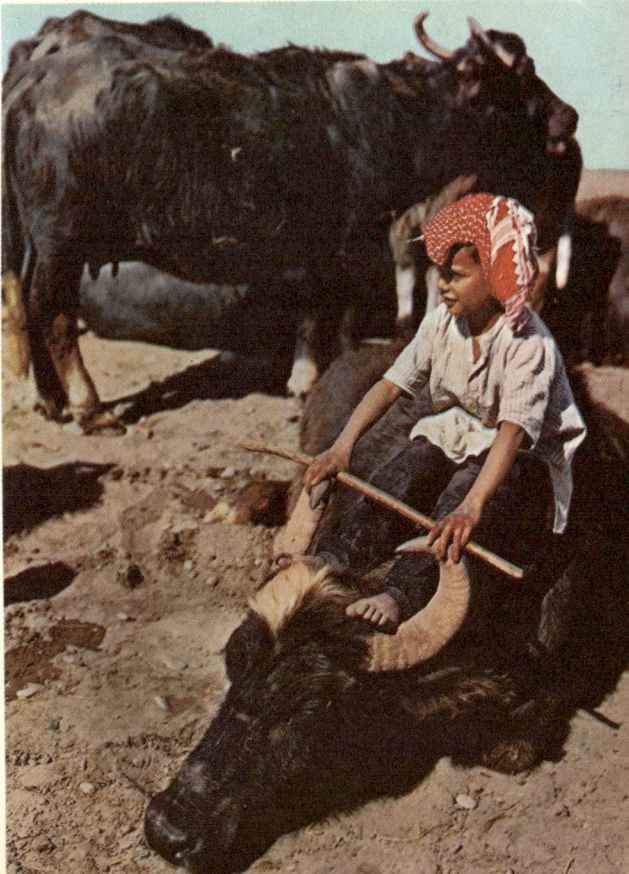

St. Basil's Cathedral on Red Square, with its onion spires, towers over Moscow.

the Mississippi River. The Kazakhs came into the area in the 1500's. Until recently many Kazakhs and Kirghiz were wandering herdsmen.

The Tadzhiks have a separate Union Republic high in the Pamir Mountains, the so-called "roof of the world." They speak a language related to Persian.

In Karelia, north of Leningrad, is a self-governing population of Karelians. They are closely related to the Finns who live in Finland. The tall, fair Estonians have a Union Republic just east of Leningrad. Both these peoples are of Finno-Ugrian stock. They speak related languages.

The Latvians and Lithuanians each have their own Union Republic on the shores of the Baltic Sea just south of Estonia. Their languages are of the same Indo-European stock from which all the principal languages of Europe descended. Lithuanian is said to be the oldest living Indo-European language. Most Estonians and Latvians are Protestants. Most Lithuanians are Roman Catholics.

The Caucasus region has three main cultural groups, each with its own Union Republic. The Georgians are a people with an old civilization. They have their own alphabet and a culture that goes back many hundred years.

The Armenians live to the south on the borders of Turkey. They have black hair, dark eyes, and rather dark skin. They too have an old civilization, with their own alphabet and a language not closely related to any other. On the shore of the Caspian Sea is the Azerbaijan Republic. Its people are of Turko-Tartar origin.

Invasions of new tribes often drove former settlers into nearby mountains for protection. For centuries the Caucasus have been a fortress for fleeing tribes. Today there are probably more different small nationality groups in the mountains of the Caucasus than there are in any other area of similar size in the world. The Khevsurs and Svans are two among many.

Mongol peoples include the Buryat Mongols, who live in the region of Lake Baikal, and the Kalmyks, who live in the north Caucasus.

Tungus peoples include the Nentsi and Evenki. They live along the Arctic coast. Until recently many were nomads who used reindeer, as do the Lapps in Lapland.

The Soviet Union has many other different peoples, each with its own language and culture. Many of the less civilized tribes have only recently received an alphabet and written language.

A peasant home in much fought-over Byelorussia, which lies between Poland and Moscow

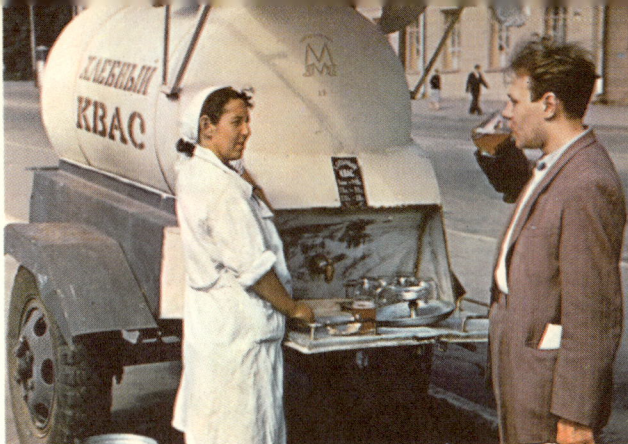

A kvass vendor makes a sale in Moscow. Kvass is a popular drink made from fermented bread.

An Uzbek man, squatting on the ground in Oriental style, enjoys a melon in the market of Samarkand.

Women helped greatly in rebuilding Stalingrad after World War II. Here they tar a road.

A Kazakh mother and child from the vast and remote Kazakh Republic in Central Asia

Peasant women of Soviet Asia. Many different peoples live in the huge Central Asia republics.

TRANSPORTATION

The Soviet Union is a land of vast distances. It needs large-scale methods of transportation.

Its broad rivers have long been important for boat and barge transport. The Volga River carries the heaviest traffic. It is navigable for 2,000 miles. Several Siberian rivers are also navigable for thousands of miles.

The northern sea route goes along the Arctic coast of the Soviet Union. It provides the fastest connection by ship with Soviet ports on the Pacific. The government has given special attention to this route. The Arctic Ocean is free of ice for two months in summer. Ships can make the run from Archangel to Vladivostok in 19 days. They stop at ports at the mouths of the rivers along the way.

Railroads are a very important means of transportation in the Soviet Union. The Russians have the longest railroad in the world, the Trans-Siberian. It runs from the Polish frontier to Vladivostok on the Pacific. The fastest trains take nine and one half days to make the trip.

The Soviet Union has now double-tracked the Trans-Siberian. It has also added another Siberian railroad. This runs to the Pacific north of Lake Baikal. In the 1930's the government built the Turk-Sib (Turkmen-Siberian) Railroad that joins Central Asia with Siberia.

Soviet Europe has many good railroad lines. The U.S.S.R. has done much to expand, improve, and electrify its rail system. In amount of freight carried, rail greatly outranks water transportation. Total railway mileage is second only to that of the United States.

Roads in the Soviet Union are rather poor. Most are not hard-surfaced and are difficult to drive on in wet weather. In recent years, however, roads have received more attention. Good automobile roads now connect many of the principal cities in Soviet Europe and certain key stretches in Soviet Asia. So few people use cars,

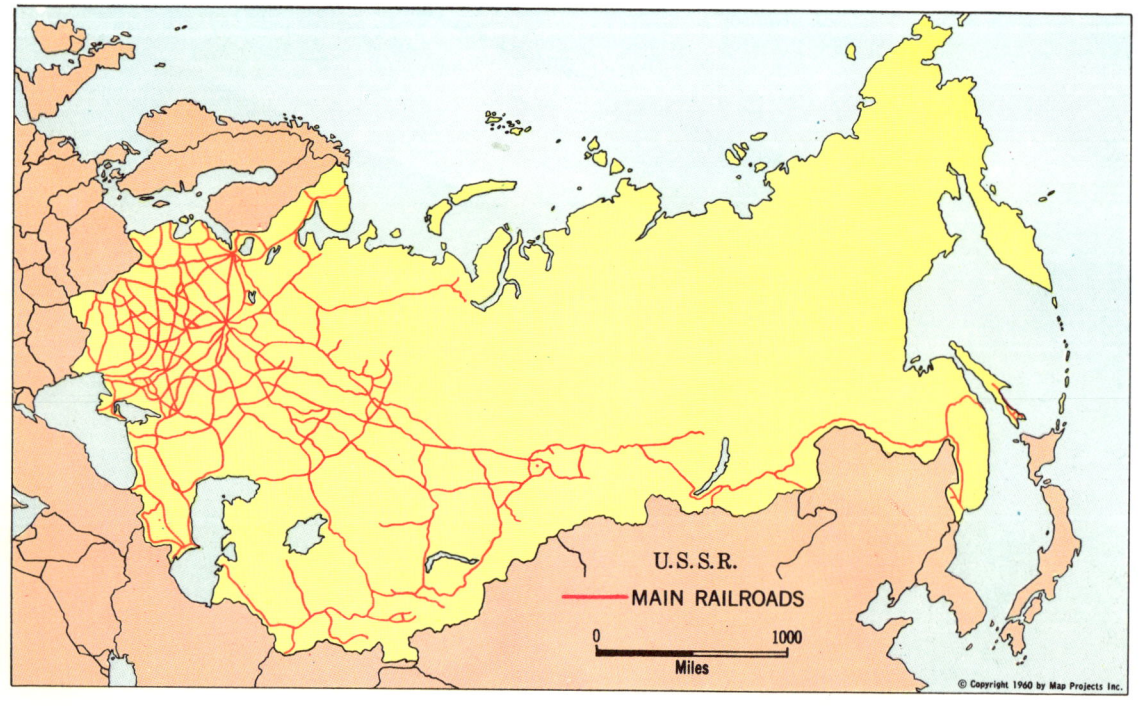

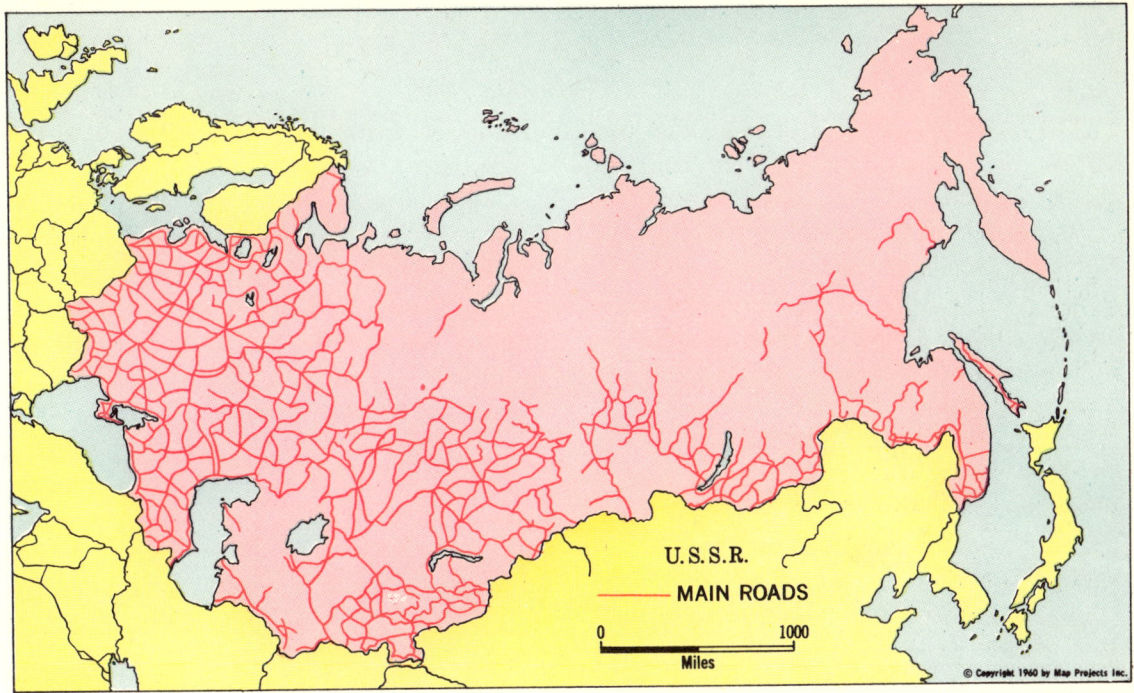

busses, and trucks that there has been little need for highways. Horses are still much used in the back country.

The Soviet Union takes a great interest in aviation. It has jumped across the centuries, so to speak, from the horse to the jet liner. Now a network of airlines joins all parts of the Union. Soviet engineers are leaders in many phases of airplane design. Their jet airliners are the largest and fastest in the world. But only a few of the Soviet people earn enough money to travel.

Moscow University towers over the city's skyline. There has been much recent building in Moscow.

SOVIET CITIES

In the old days the Soviet Union was a land of many farms and few cities. Now it is a land of fewer, but larger, farms and many cities.

First is Moscow, the capital of the U.S.S.R. and the fifth largest city in the world. It is the seat of government, and an important center of art, science, manufacturing, and trade. Canals now connect Moscow with the Baltic and Black Seas.

Leningrad, the second largest city in the Union, has 3,300,000 people. It was formerly St. Petersburg, Czar Peter the Great's "window on Europe." It has many historical buildings. Like Moscow, it is a center of art, science, and manufacturing. It is located 400 miles northwest of Moscow, on the delta of the Neva River.

Gorky, Kalinin, Kuibyshev, and Saratov are other important cities in the Russian

Ancient Kiev on the west bank of the Dnieper River is the third largest city in the Soviet Union.

Republic. They are ancient river trading centers, now with many industries as well.

Historic Kiev is the capital of the Ukraine. When it was a former capital of Russia, it was called "Holy Kiev" because of its churches and monasteries. It sits on a high bank overlooking the Dnieper River. Other important Ukrainian cities are Kharkov, a great industrial and trading center, and Odessa, a historic Black Sea port.

Stalingrad, a huge industrial center on the lower Volga, will be long remembered as the city that stopped the Nazis, whose attacking armies finally surrendered in January 1943. This marked a turning-point of World War II.

The trading and industrial centers of Omsk, Tomsk, and Irkutsk are well-known Siberian cities. Vladivostok, eight days east of Moscow by train, is Russia's chief Pacific port.

Tashkent, Bokhara, and Samarkand are ancient cities in Central Asia. They were once important trade centers on caravan routes. Today factories have become part of the landscape of these cities.

The names of the big new cities of Magnitogorsk, Komsomolsk, Frunze, Stalinabad, and Karaganda were almost unknown two decades ago. Now each of them has a population of well over 100,000. There are many other new cities developing the iron and copper and coal of the Urals and Soviet Asia. They are producing the minerals and fuel upon which the industrial strength of the Soviet Union depends.

Leningrad, the U.S.S.R.'s leading port, was built in 1703 to give Russia access to the Atlantic.

FARMING

In spite of its huge size, only a comparatively small part of the Soviet Union is suitable for agriculture. Most of Central Asia is too dry. The marshes of Byelorussia are too wet. In the north the growing season is too short. In northeastern Siberia the ground is too cold. In some places the soil is better for forests than for farms.

The good farm land is quite thickly settled. Therefore, the simplest way to get more crops is to work the good land better. That is why the government became interested in collective farming.

According to Communist theory, land and industries should be owned by the state, not by private individuals or companies. This, it was thought, would help bring about socialism, the first step toward communism. In the revolution of 1917, therefore, the government took over the land and industries.

Workers in the factories of czarist Russia felt that almost any change would

Huge wheatfields stretch away into the distance on the collective farms of the Ukraine.

Sunflowers are a favorite crop. Soviet citizens munch sunflower seeds just as Americans eat peanuts.

Many goats are raised on the upland pastures of the Caucasus in the Georgian Republic.

be for the better. They supported the new system. But it was different in the countryside. There the big estates of the nobles had been divided among the farmers. These farmers tended to look upon the land that they worked as their own private property.

The Soviet government felt that to keep power and to strengthen the nation, more industries were necessary. For those industries the cities needed more workers, and more food for those workers.

But the land was divided into small farms. They were too small for farm machinery. And these farms were being divided into smaller farms as the population grew. Labor was staying on the farm instead of coming to the cities to work in factories. The farmers were not sending enough food to the cities.

The government thought that collective farms would solve this problem. A collective farm is a large farm formed from many small individual farms. It is often all the land of one village, or of a group of villages. It is big enough to use machines. Land formerly wasted in fence rows can be plowed. It should therefore produce more food with less work. Laborers no longer needed on the farm could come to the city and work in the new factories. Furthermore, it was hoped, a collective farmer would stop thinking about making money for himself and start thinking about producing more for the state.

A collective farm does offer some advantages to the farmer. These include regular hours of labor, less hand labor, and some insurance against crop failure. The government promised that collective farms would also have better schools, hospitals, and so forth. But, of course, collective farms have some very real disadvantages.

In the Kirghiz Republic of Central Asia much newly-irrigated land is planted with cotton.

278 U.S.S.R.

Many farmers, particularly the more prosperous, did not like the idea of giving up their own individual farms. They fought against the attempts of the government to set up collectives. The government put great pressure on the farmers to join collectives. There was a bitter struggle. Rich farmers lost their property. Many farmers starved to death.

Finally, in the 1930's, the government won. Today four fifths of the agricultural land in the Soviet Union has been collectivized. The rest is in farms operated by the state. There are no more privately owned farms.

Collective farm land is worked by the village farmers according to a plan they develop themselves. This plan, however, must be approved by the state. And, in reality, all decisions on what and how much to plant, extra work, and so forth, are made by the government. The collective farmers elect their own director. There are various specialists, technicians, mechanics, and clerical workers. The rest of the people work outside on the farm property.

Payment is determined by how many workday units a person gives the farm. Skilled workers get more than unskilled. For instance, an unskilled farm worker might get one workday unit for eight hours of work. A soil scientist or dairy specialist might get two or three workday units for each eight hours of his work. Most of the harvest goes to the state at fixed prices. The rest is sold on the free collective farm market at higher prices.

Some income goes to the state for taxes. Some goes to pay necessary expenses. Some is held in reserve. The remainder is divided among the members of the collective farm.

These people live on a collective farm in Byelorussia, a republic noted for its flax.

The large state farms of the U.S.S.R. are managed by men such as these in the Ukraine.

Every collective farm has a day nursery to free parents of young children for work.

Stacking straw on a Ukrainian collective farm. Soviet scientists are studying new uses for it.

Professor Sokolov is one of Russia's foremost developers of new varieties of corn.

It is divided on the basis of how many workday units each member earned. Some payment is in cash, some in farm products. If crops are good, everybody benefits. If they are poor, everyone is affected. But even in the best of years, Soviet farmers earn far less than American farmers.

Each collective farmer also has his own small plot of ground on which he can keep a few animals and chickens. He can also raise his own vegetables, fruits, or bees. He can sell them on the collective farm market and keep the income for himself.

Another type of farm is the state farm. State farms occupy one fifth of the farm land in the Soviet Union. A state farm is like a factory, operated by a manager and workers on fixed salaries. State farms are usually larger than collective farms.

All the crops and livestock of the Soviet Union are now raised on either collective or state farms. Production has gone up. Yield per acre is still less than in many parts of the Western world, but it is increasing.

Wheat and rye are the great grain crops of the Soviet Union. Corn and potatoes are also widely grown. Oats and barley are raised where it is too cold or dry for wheat. Cotton and fruits grow on the irrigated fields of Central Asia.

The valleys and foothills of the Caucasus and the shores of the Black Sea are the only subtropical parts of the Soviet Union.

Russia still depends a great deal on human muscle. Here women shovel wheat with wooden shovels.

There farmers raise tea, grapes, and citrus crops. On the drier plains east of the Volga, in Siberia, and in Central Asia, herdsmen raise cattle, sheep, and horses.

Flax is grown in Byelorussia and around Moscow. Sugar beets grow in the Ukraine, the Caucasus, Central Asia, and the Soviet Far East. Grapes grow in the south.

Soviet scientists do much experimental work in agriculture. They have developed fast-ripening crops for the Arctic.

In spite of all the discussion it has aroused, collective farming is in the Soviet Union to stay. It is without question a significant development in the history of the Soviet economy.

The new Volga dam at Stalingrad will produce more electric power than any other dam in the world.

THE SOVIETS' EXPANDING INDUSTRY

The Soviet Union, next to the United States, is the world's greatest industrial power. But this was not always so. In 1913, before World War I, Russia was a backward country. The small amount of industry it had suffered greatly in the war, the revolution of 1917, and the civil war that followed.

Not till 1928 did industry get back to the 1913 level. Then the government started a series of five-year plans. Its hope was to catch up with the most advanced nations. Industry took big steps forward.

World War II, however, set back this program. But since the war the Soviet Union has made much progress. The amount of goods it produces for each person is still lower than in the Western European countries. But the total produced is greater than in any other country except the United States. In the field of technical science, the Soviet Union is very advanced. In rockets it leads the world.

In order to strengthen the nation, the U.S.S.R. first developed its heavy industry, that is, its coal, steel, and metals. Upon these all other industries, transportation, and defense depend. So the government put them ahead of consumer goods. Steel came before housing, shoes, clothes, and toys. Many consumer goods are still scarce, and they are far more expensive than in the United States.

The principal center of heavy industry in Soviet Europe is the Donets Basin, or Donbas, in the southern Ukraine. Here are large coal mines. Nearby is high-grade iron ore from Krivoi Rog. Steel is produced at Stalino and other centers. The Donbas cities specialize in various metal products.

Another iron and steel center has arisen at Kharkov, "the Chicago of the Soviet Union," in the Ukraine. Its manufactures include tractors, trucks, and heavy industrial machinery.

During the first five-year plan, five new factory cities were built at Stalingrad along the lower Volga. Today there are many

A giant Soviet steel mill. Soviet steel production ranks second to that of the United States.

more. Important among them are plants for tractors and trucks.

The Communists very early started building dams for hydroelectric power. A famous one was constructed by an American engineer at Dniepropetrovsk on the Dnieper River in the Ukraine in the 1930's. It was destroyed by the Nazis, but rebuilt after the war.

Near it rose the city of Zaporozhe for the production of aluminum. Such production needs lots of cheap power. This is obtained from electricity produced at Dniepropetrovsk. Many other hydroelectric stations have been built in different parts of the country. The largest in the world has just been put into operation at Kuibyshev on the Volga.

Moscow and Leningrad are important centers of industry. Moscow is noted for ball bearings, automobiles, and textiles. The chief textile production of the Soviet Union takes place in Moscow and in an area to the northeast.

Leningrad is known for machine tools, chemicals, electrical goods, and trucks. It is also the largest publishing center in the Soviet Union.

At the junction of the Oka and Volga Rivers lies the important trading center of Gorky. It is noted for the manufacture of automobiles and river steamers. Automobiles are also made at Yaroslavl to the north. Other river steamers are built at Kiev on the Dnieper. Ocean-going vessels are built at Leningrad and Odessa.

Tula for metals and Voronezh for machinery are other large manufacturing cities in European Russia. Archangel, in the northern forest belt, is an important lumber town.

Baku, on the Caspian Sea, with both wells and refineries, is the oldest oil center in the U.S.S.R. It was once the largest. But a new field near Kuibyshev on the middle Volga now produces more. Oil is also found in the north Caucasus.

The Soviet Union is rich in other minerals. In the Kola Peninsula in the north is the world's largest supply of apatite. This is used as a source of phosphate for fertilizer.

The U.S.S.R. also has the world's greatest supply of manganese, a mineral needed in steel production. Manganese ore is mined in the southern Ukraine and northern Caucasus. Much of it is exported.

In recent years more attention has been given to consumer goods. There are still severe shortages, especially in automobiles and housing. New housing has never been

Much of the heavy work in the Soviet Union, such as road maintenance, is done by women.

Julien Bryan—Photo Researchers

Buildings such as this new apartment house in Leningrad are going up in many Soviet cities.

Julien Bryan—Photo Researchers

J. D. Winbray—Shostal

Inside a Soviet textile factory. Many textile plants have been built recently in Central Asia.

Paul Hufner—Shostal

One of the Soviet's largest textile mills is in Tashkent, capital of the Uzbek Republic.

able to keep up with the rapid growth of the cities. But one of the typical sights in the Soviet Union is the rows of new workers' apartments in towns and cities almost everywhere.

The Soviet Union has a State Planning Board. This board makes the overall plans for the location of industry, building of factories, and scheduling of production. This is a basic part of the Soviet's "planned economy."

In a country as large as the U.S.S.R. there are, of course, many other minerals, resources, and industries. Since there is such a shortage of consumer goods, and since the government wants to catch up with other countries, industry is very active. Almost all branches are growing rapidly. More factories are going up all the time. What is lonely farm land one year is often a new industrial town the next.

Modern collective farm tractors on display at an agricultural exhibit in Moscow

John Strohm

A self-propelled combine—a product of the stepped-up Soviet farm machinery program

John Strohm

Cows on a Siberian collective farm. The Soviets are stressing increased cattle production.

SIBERIAN PIONEER LANDS

Siberia and Soviet Asia are to the Soviet Union what the West was to the United States a hundred years ago. They are the great pioneer lands.

Like our Great Plains the western Siberian Plain is wide and flat. Much of it is cattle country and wheat fields. Novosibirsk is the largest city.

Until recently vast areas in southwestern Siberia and the northern Kazakh Republic had never been plowed. Rainfall there was low. But scientists thought it might be enough for crops, if dry land farming methods were used. Since 1954 some 87,500,000 acres have been put to the plow in these "virgin lands."

In the Ural Mountains is the second largest industrial center in the Union. The Urals are among the richest in minerals of any mountains in the world. They contain iron, copper, nickel, platinum, and many other ores. Because of Ural ores the U.S.S.R. holds first place in world production of magnesite and chromium.

Coal from Karaganda in the Kazakh Republic helps make steel in the Ural blast furnaces of Magnitogorsk, Nizhni Tagil, and Zlatoust. Degtyarka, also in the Urals, is a copper mining city. Sverdlovsk has a large copper smelter and a machine-tool factory. Chelyabinsk makes tractors for the collective farms of Siberia.

The Soviets are opening up another big industrial center in the Kuznetsk Basin (Kuzbas). This is in the upper Yenisei Valley in Siberia. Here are the Soviet Union's largest coal reserves. Stalinsk is the center of a steel industry using this coal and iron ore from mountains to the south.

Siberia's rivers offer great possibilities for development. A giant power dam has been built at Irkutsk on the Angara River, and others have been planned.

Bears and other game abound in Siberia's forests.

The Soviet Union's chief source of gold used to be along the Lena River. Recently gold was also found on two other rivers nearby. These are all in the huge and remote Yakut Republic, one third the size of the United States. Soviet gold production is second only to that of South Africa.

Another important area is the Soviet Far East. Farmers are tilling new collective farms along the valley of the mighty Amur River. Fine stands of timber cover the many mountains. Khabarovsk is a large trading and manufacturing city. Komsomolsk is a great steel center.

The Soviet Union contains the largest forest in the world outside the tropics. From Finland to the Pacific—but mostly in Siberia—pine, spruce, larch, and fir cover one and a half billion acres. There are sawmills at Igarka on the Yenisei and at other river ports. Some of the timber is good for saw lumber and pulpwood. Part of this lumber and pulpwood is exported to timber-poor countries.

Sakhalin Island in the Pacific has oil wells and coal mines. Important mineral deposits are found at other places in Siberia. In many of them development has just begun. Geologists think there are many more still to be discovered.

Jerry Cooke—Photo Researchers

This new dam across the Angara River will furnish power for Siberia's growing industries.

A Siberian village often has an unpaved main street and a rough, pioneer appearance.

Jerry Cooke—Photo Researchers

A Soviet science laboratory. The U.S.S.R. offers its citizens a great deal of science education.

THE FUTURE OF THE SOVIET UNION

The largest and one of the richest countries in the world should have a good future. What will it be?

Some things we can be pretty sure of. Siberia, for instance, will continue to develop, particularly in the Urals, and Kuzbas. Further hydroelectric developments are planned for the Angara and other Siberian rivers. These will enormously increase industrial development in these areas.

Soviet scientists will pay increasing attention in the future to the permafrost area. They will try to make it more productive and easier to live in. They will develop crops that can better stand cold, drought, and shorter growing seasons.

Irrigation in Central Asia will reclaim more deserts. The Soviets will also continue to develop their Arctic coast and islands. As use of the northern sea route grows, ports near the mouths of Siberian rivers will become more important.

Atomic power will be widely applied, especially in sections of the U.S.S.R. where coal and hydroelectric power are lacking.

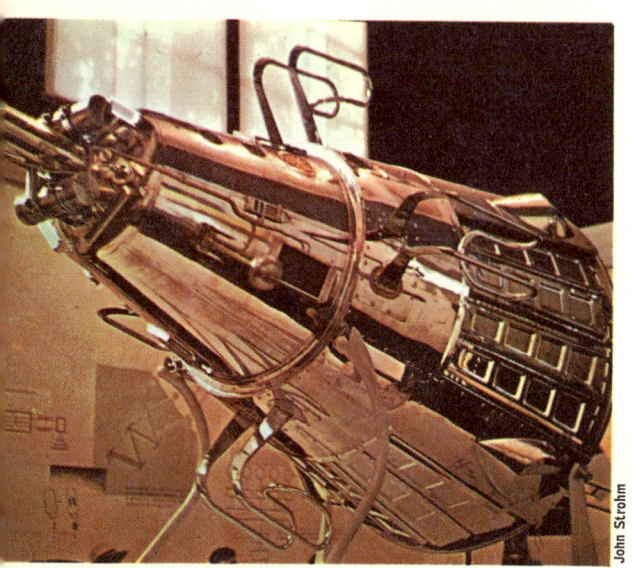

This is the nose cone of a Soviet space satellite on exhibition at a trade fair in Moscow.

The apartment shortage in the Soviet Union will be relieved by new housing in major cities.

Jerry Cooke—Photo Researchers

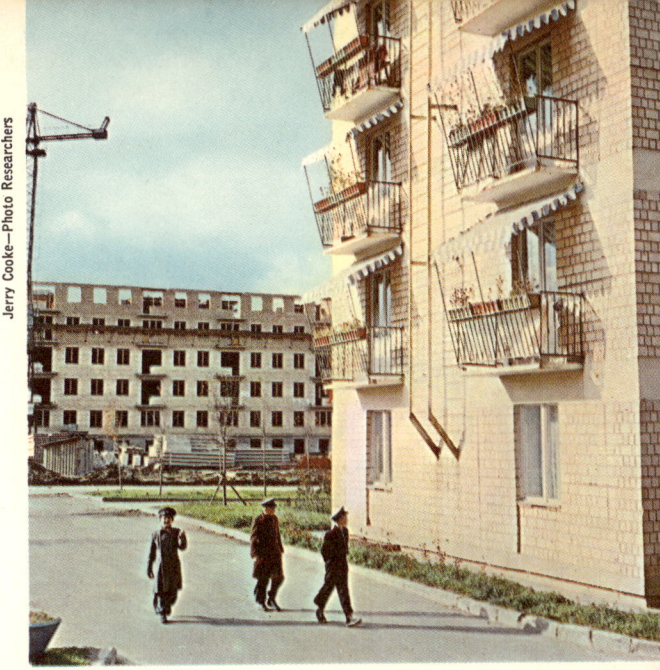

The rapid development of the Soviet Union and the countries of Eastern Europe is a challenge to the United States. Asia, Africa, and much of Latin America are not industrialized. The people in those lands are poor, often very poor. They will follow anyone who promises them a better living.

The Soviet Union is making great efforts to persuade these people and, indeed, all the world, to follow its way of life. It offers the people of the underdeveloped lands more food and clothes; schools; hospitals; and new industries if they will adopt Communism. But the Communist way of life is a dictatorship. There are none of the civil and political freedoms that we know and value so highly.

The United States also offers the people of the underdeveloped lands a chance to have a better life. We, too, offer them ways to get more food and clothing, to have schools and medical care, to build up industries which will provide jobs and consumer goods for more people. And we offer them a way to get these good things without losing their freedom. In fact, they should gain greater freedom. Will these nations follow our way or the Soviet way? That is one of the great issues facing the world in the years ahead.

Russia's future lies with children like these "Young Pioneers" hiking through Moscow.

John Strohm

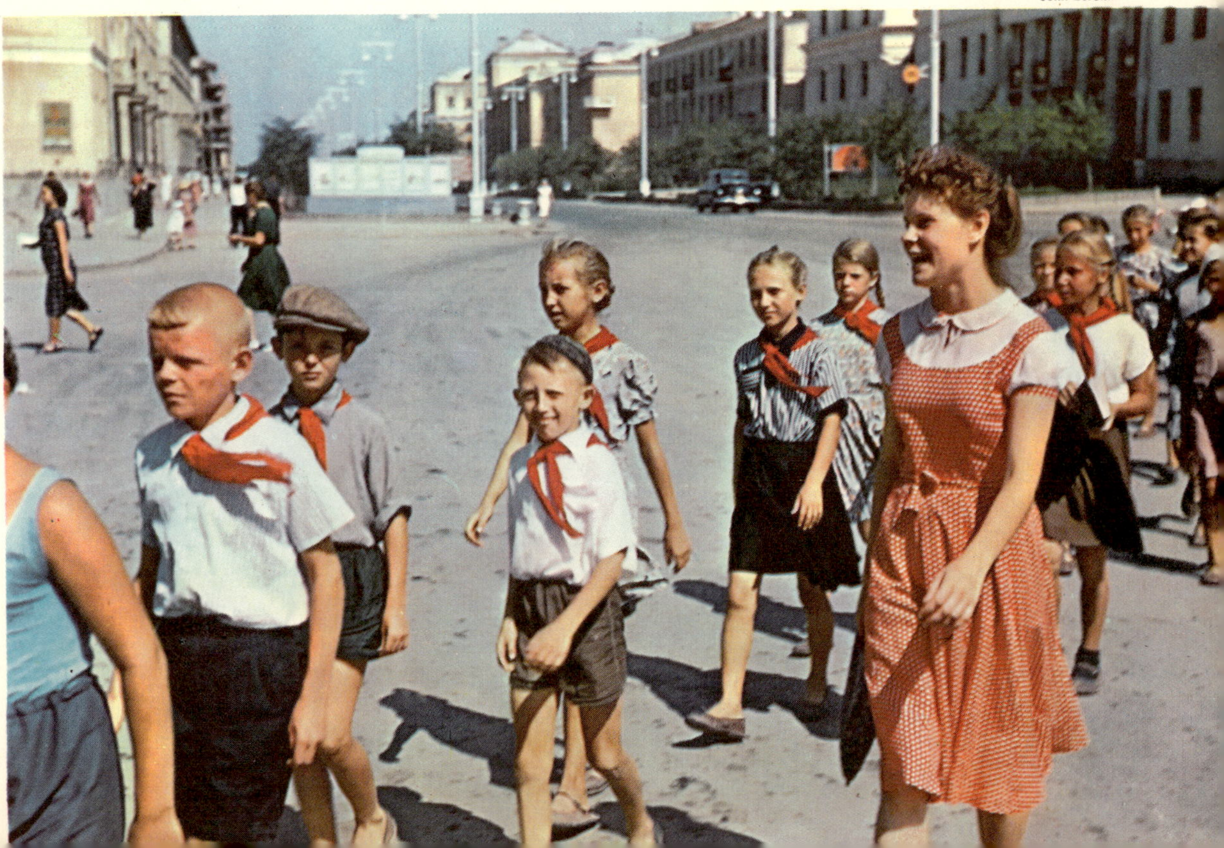

EUROPE AND THE U.S.S.R.—FACTS AND FIGURES

PRINCIPAL COUNTRIES: AREA AND POPULATION

Country	Area in sq. miles	Population (est. 1960)
Albania	10,800	1,590,500
Austria	32,375	7,144,400
Belgium	11,799	9,224,200
Bulgaria	42,796	7,905,000
Czechoslovakia	49,354	13,872,000
Denmark	16,576	4,601,900
Finland	130,100	4,502,600
France	212,660	45,600,300
Germany, East	41,537	17,689,600
Germany, West	95,300	54,980,000
Great Britain and Northern Ireland	94,250	52,832,000
Greece	51,182	8,355,800
Hungary	35,912	10,078,600
Iceland	39,750	178,000
Ireland (Eire)	27,137	2,912,900
Italy	116,270	49,991,100
Luxembourg	998	325,100
Netherlands	13,025	11,588,400
Norway	125,100	3,607,300
Poland	120,359	30,069,000
Portugal	35,400	9,303,400
Romania	91,700	18,567,500
Spain	194,945	30,425,800
Sweden	173,430	7,546,500
Switzerland	15,944	5,329,100
U.S.S.R.	8,599,600	214,020,000
Yugoslavia	98,900	18,775,800

LARGE CITIES AND THEIR POPULATION

City and Country	Est. Pop.
London, Great Britain	8,222,340
Moscow, U.S.S.R.	5,032,000
Leningrad, U.S.S.R.	2,888,000
Paris, France	2,850,190
Berlin (West), West Germany	2,228,000
Rome, Italy	1,894,540
Madrid, Spain	1,887,160
Hamburg, West Germany	1,786,775
Vienna, Austria	1,766,100
Barcelona, Spain	1,431,570
Milan, Italy	1,403,210
Athens, Greece	1,378,590
Brussels, Belgium	1,308,830
Bucharest, Romania	1,237,000
Berlin (East), East Germany	1,174,580
Budapest, Hungary	1,164,960
Naples, Italy	1,125,582
Birmingham, Great Britain	1,110,800
Glasgow, Great Britain	1,095,030
Warsaw, Poland	1,081,000
Munich, West Germany	1,001,830

PRINCIPAL MOUNTAINS AND THEIR ELEVATIONS

Mountain and Country	Height in feet
Stalin, U.S.S.R.	24,590
Lenin, U.S.S.R.	23,380
Elbrus, U.S.S.R.	18,480
Klyuchevskaya, U.S.S.R.	15,912
Mont Blanc, France	15,780
Weisshorn, Switzerland	14,800
Matterhorn, Switzerland	14,701
Etna, Italy	10,705

PRINCIPAL LAKES AND THEIR AREAS

Lake and Region	Area in sq. miles
Caspian Sea, U.S.S.R.	169,380
Aral Sea, U.S.S.R.	25,400
Baikal, U.S.S.R.	12,670
Ladoga, U.S.S.R.	7,100
Balkhash, U.S.S.R.	6,900
Onega, U.S.S.R.	3,800
Vaner, Northern Europe	2,150
Peipus, U.S.S.R.	1,400

PRINCIPAL RIVERS AND THEIR LENGTH

River and Region	Length in miles
Lena, U.S.S.R.	2,800
Amur, U.S.S.R.	2,700
Yenisei, U.S.S.R.	2,430
Ob, U.S.S.R.	2,260
Volga, U.S.S.R.	2,250
Danube, Western-Eastern Europe	1,770
Ural, U.S.S.R.	1,530
Dnieper, U.S.S.R.	1,420
Rhine, Western Europe	820
Elbe, Western-Eastern Europe	720
Rhone, Western Europe	505
Seine, Western Europe	482